Worknado

Reimagining the way you work to live

Shane Rodgers

Copyright © 2023 Shane Rodgers

All rights reserved. No part of this book may be copied, reproduced, or transmitted in any form without the prior written permission of the author.

ISBN: 9798355398279

Cover image: Craig Mann

Dedicated to everyone who ever believed in me and all the ancestors who survived long enough so I could be born.

"Don't only practice your art, but force your way into its secrets, for it and knowledge can raise men to the divine."
  - **Ludwig van Beethoven** (German composer)

"The people who are crazy enough to think they can change the world are the ones who do."
  - **Steve Jobs** (Entrepreneur and co-founder of Apple)

CONTENTS

	Introduction	8
1	**If I could turn back time**	14
	1. The career advice I wish I had at 25	15
	2. More career advice I wish I had earlier	22
2	**Reimagining your career**	32
	1. It is never too late to reboot	32
	2. Getting your groove back at work	35
	3. Making better use of your time	44
	4. Money – how much do you really need?	48
	5. Why certain people get ahead	52
	6. Secrets of people who snare great jobs	60
	7. Repackaging yourself for success	69
	8. Building your personal brand	73
	9. The myths of career progression	78
	10. Avoiding the biggest career mistakes	85
	11. Facing fear and taking risks	89
	12. Making decisions in a half right world	93
	13. Fixing problems by changing your vantage point	96
3	**Recapturing your life balance**	99
	1. The work and life divide	99
	2. It only takes one thing	102
	3. The death of the twilight zone	105
	4. Time – our most precious gift	108
	5. Breaking out of a rut	109
	6. The life advice I wish I had at 25	113

	7. Simple ways to better days	127
	8. Getting through really tough days	131
	9. Living a life of no regrets	141
	10. Learning to believe in yourself	145
	11. Giving yourself permission to rest	148
	12. Giving yourself permission to be happy	150
	13. Overcoming the curse of busyness	154
	14. Freeing yourself from the competition	157
4	**Riding the waves of change**	159
	1. The forces reshaping our working lives	159
	2. The COVID-19 blip	167
	3. The rise of stretch jobs	171
	4. Rising trends in the new job market	173
	5. Innovation and incubation	177
	6. Fractured pathways	183
	7. The end of agism?	189
	8. Video killed the meeting room star	194
	9. The gender tragedy	197
	10. Why are we so afraid of part-time work?	202
	11. Workspaces	206
	12. Work cultures for the new world	211
	13. The traits of great leaders	217
	14. The search for truth	224
5	**Finding the life you imagined**	230
	1. Avoiding burnout	231
	2. The meaning of life	236
	3. Working out why you were put on Earth	241

Then came the Worknado…

There is a quiet rumbling, rolling like a gathering thunder through our workplaces, our homes, and our lives in general.

The Worknado has been building for a while, and now it is here.

This book looks at the rising forces of change in our workplaces, intermingled with insights from years of experience managing people and seeking to understand the secret languages of the workplace.

Ever since our societies carved an ambition beyond subsistence living, work has become our obsession, largely dictating our standard of living and our sense of identity.

For generations, our concepts of work have conformed to patterns built largely off parameters set in the industrial age to balance employee and employer needs. Heavy inertia has anchored the workplace status quo.

As we move deeper into the 21st century, the mood for change is palpable. The rigidity of our workplace systems and the long-accepted conventions of employment are being seriously questioned.

The most obvious driver of this is the digital native "Millennial" generation, with a different mindset and a profound scepticism about the type of lives accepted by their parents and grandparents.

But the mood for change is deeper than that. It goes to older people with fresh energy who are not willing to fade away from society. It captures women who are no longer prepared to accept lip service around equality.

It comes from men and women watching their lives slip away as they feel trapped and soulless. It emanates from parents watching time stealing childhoods and never giving them back. It arises in professional occupations where bizarre and illogical expectations have emerged around very long hours and "face-time" in the office.

While the rumblings of dissatisfaction are not new, between 2020 and 2023 they grew louder and closer. The COVID-19 pandemic finally gave us permission to discuss different ways of working and living without feeling like Oliver Twist's orphan Oliver asking for more. As a result, we are having real conversations about part-time work, multi-jobs, jobs that stretch across different vocations, working from anywhere and creating workplaces better tuned to multi-generations.

I started writing this book long before the pandemic. COVID-19 has merely added a booster rocket to forces that were already building around us.

We stand at a crucial historical juncture blessed with a real opportunity to enhance human life and grasp a different, better future. Work as we know it may never be the same again.

- Shane Rodgers

Introduction

Sometimes, late at night, you find yourself with some clear air. Away from the clutter, your mind discovers the space to think, to pull some strands together and provide just a few moments of clarity.

That happened to me late one Saturday night in 2015 as I sat with a single glass of red wine trying to make sense of this crazy little thing called life.

It was the first time in a long time I had really stopped to think. I thought about how quickly the years from 25 to 50 had passed. I thought about what I knew then compared to what I know now. And, just for an instant, I wished I could go back and talk to my 25-year-old self. I barely knew that guy anymore, but I hoped he would trust me enough to listen to a few things I had learnt in the years since.

A few minutes later I started writing an article called *The Career Advice I Wish I Had at 25*. Less than an hour after that the article was done and posted onto the LinkedIn social media platform, complete with a picture of myself and my eldest daughter Danielle, I went off to sleep feeling very relaxed and calm - that serene feeling you get when you have something off your chest.

I had written quite a few blogs on LinkedIn, but I knew by the following morning that there was something special about this one. By morning (yes, on a Saturday night) it had been read thousands of times. And the viralling has never stopped.

The article has been read millions of times on LinkedIn, cut and pasted onto hundreds of other websites and printed out and stuck on walls all over the world. It has taken on a life of its own and it is still being passed around like one of those giant inflatable balls at a sporting event.

People regularly contact me to say the article has changed their lives and I am constantly amazed at what people read into it when they view my comments from the vantage point of their own contexts.

So, I got thinking again…

The response was not just about an article and a few random late-night reflections. It had hit a nerve and surfaced a feeling secretly harboured by millions of people around the world – something is wrong with the way many (maybe most) people are approaching work and, by extension, their lives.

Too many people are always in a rush, working ridiculous hours, putting in "face time" because it is expected of them, deprioritising things that really matter, moving into the red zone of stress and anxiety, and burning out.

There are many reasons for this. The pace of economic and corporate disruption has been in hyperdrive for many years. As a result, few jobs provide genuine long-term stability and redundancy has become a career status rather than a rare event in poor economic cycles. There are lots of other reasons discussed elsewhere in this book.

It feels like we are on a historically significant social and economic change period and the work and careers that support our lives are at the epicentre of this. We are moving into an era in which careers might last 70 years. Robots and automation will remove many more manual tasks and progressively take over some intelligent tasks as well. Increasing numbers of people will have multi-job careers rather than a single job and more people (at least in Western countries) will be self-employed or work in unconventional environments. The very nature of what most humans do to make a living will be disrupted.

Perhaps even more importantly, the options to fill our days will keep growing. But there will never be more than 24 hours in a day. The pressure to do too much has the potential to wear us down if we do not learn to prioritise and to get those priorities right.

As the world emerged from the palpable weirdness of the global pandemic we heard a lot about the "great resignation" as a lockdown-weary workforce sought solace and serendipity in change.

The disruption resulted in real conversations about hybrid work and deep, genuine flexibility that simply would not have happened in the past.

People who considered full-time work their inevitable lot in life are running the ruler over part-time or portfolio careers that create variety and lustre in their weeks.

Many are finally biting the bullet and doing complete career changes or chasing the dream they have long harboured.

The newfound effectiveness of video communication has, in many occupations and companies, taken geography off the table.

Companies are reviewing their underutilised workspaces and seeking radical and creative thinking on what offices should really look like in a post-pandemic world. Some have abandoned them completely.

Even though it took the pandemic to give everyone permission to even have these conversations, the fact that the thinking has been embraced so readily reveals some of the quiet desperation that had crept into our modes of existence:

- People seeing their children grow only in bursts between long days and travel, with memories full of missing milestones.
- People battling guilt in every aspect of their lives – not enough time at home, not enough time at work if you want to get ahead.
- Lives full of dreams and promises that are strangled slowly by the reality of meeting your obligations, ticking all the boxes, eating well enough and getting enough sleep.
- Sitting in slow-moving traffic daydreaming about the beach, sitting in the train as it stops every three minutes on the slow roll home, slowly sinking into a societal proforma styled from years of convenient conformity.

People fear that when they hit a certain stage in life they start to stand still. Life still seems to move around you, but inertia captures you in one spot or on one path.

There is nowhere to stop, rethink and reset. Time carries us along rather than giving us space to call a time-out and shake up the program.

The moment in time we have now, gifted largely through adversity and new challenges, is the first time in a very long time that we have the space and attention to really think about how we as humans should be living at this stage in history.

It is an empowering opportunity and a challenge to really push back on our comfort zones and re-calibrate our priorities.

When history is written about this period, it probably will not be about the "great resignation". Instead, historians and social researchers will likely plot a time when we threw it all up in the air and put it back together a different way.

This may be more than a small conversation about working from home and flexibility. We may well be at the dawn of a new age of human enlightenment.

Inside this Worknado that is upon us, we need to re-imagine the way we work to live.

Our lives and our society are crying out for a reset button so we can restore a feeling that we are back in control, not just constantly staving off chaos.

I have been a manager, writer and business executive since I was in my twenties, but I do not claim to have the answers. This book merely shares observations in the hope that some of the things I have noticed over time will resonate with others, or at least give comfort that many of the things we feel, and experience, are also experienced by others.

I have included research and examples in parts to back my thoughts, but this book is designed to be more of a personal reflection than a formal text on the modern workplace.

It is also my version of a time machine for my 25-year-old self. Perhaps we will be able to time-travel books well before we can send people.

A colleague once said that if we cannot be a good example for our children, we should at least be a terrible warning. Hopefully this book does a bit of both.

SECTION 1

If I could turn back time

"You can't turn back time. But you can wind it up again."
- **Bonnie Prudden**
(Physical fitness pioneer)

This section is based purely on personal experience and observations from the past quarter century. I have been fortunate enough to be in senior management roles since my mid-twenties and to have worked in about 20 different workplaces during that time. I have supervised hundreds of people, watched careers rise and fall, read thousands of resumes and observed the people who are happy in their work and those who are miserable.

Time is a wonderful teacher. It shows us many scenarios and equips us with insights on how they might play out. It reminds us that all things are fleeting if you give them enough time. The forces of day-to-day life can easily distract us from the things that matter most and lure us into an underlived life operating on automatic pilot. This section outlines the many career lessons that would have been useful when I was starting out.

1. The career advice I wish I had at 25

It seems apt to begin the *Worknado* journey with the article that spawned the idea. *The career advice I wish I had at 25* has been read more than six million times and continues to bounce around the world. It goes like this…

In the future, when we turn 50, we will each be given a ticket to a time machine and, just once, we will be able to go back in time and talk to our 25-year-old selves.

Even then, time travel will be expensive and wreak havoc with frequent flyer programs. So there will only be one trip. What if we could? What would we say? What advice would we give?

I often wish I could do this. Just once. So, just in case the time machine ever comes along, this is the career advice I would give my 25-year-old self.

A career is a marathon, not a sprint

Chill. When we are younger, we tend to be impatient. As you get older you realise there is no real rush. Life, and the careers we pursue to fill it and pay the bills, needs to be approached on a long-term basis. If you sprint you will wear out or start to resent work that you previously enjoyed. Allow yourself time to breathe and grow. Things will come if you work hard and allow yourself time to get good at things. Always rushing only leaves you empty, and tired. It is fine to give yourself permission to take some time in the slow lane with the hat people. You will find yourself seeing things that you didn't realise were there.

Most success comes from repetition, not new things

I remember high profile Australian hairdressing magnate Stefan Ackerie telling me this in 2003. I had never really thought about it before. A few years later Malcolm Gladwell's brilliant book *Outliers* was published, promoting the idea that you needed to spend 10,000 hours on something to become truly expert at it. This applied to the Beatles and their Hamburg gigs and Bill Gates who, through a series of fortuitous accidents, ended up spending more time than almost anyone else on a computer.

The lesson here is get good at things before you try to move to the next thing. Genuine expertise belongs to an elite few. They seldom have superpowers. They usually have endurance, patience and take a long-term view. They also love what they do. If you find that, don't let it go.

If work was really so great all the rich people would have the jobs

It is well established that almost nobody laments on their death bed that they did not spend enough time at the office. This seems obvious. Yet still we let contrived circumstances and fairly trivial issues keep us from important events like school sport days and our kids getting badges for picking up rubbish. I can remember pretty much every sport day and certificate presentation I missed. I cannot remember any of the reasons that I missed them.

Deprioritise your career when your kids are young

If you have skills, commitment and passion, careers tend to take care of themselves. Over the long haul, it really doesn't matter if you have a few years when your career is in canter mode while you prioritise young children. Some time ago I was watching some video of my kids when they were little and I realised, again, that the little people in that video don't exist in that form anymore. They have grown into pride-worthy adults but the tiny people with wonder in their eyes were just passing through. If you miss that time meeting deadlines and finishing reports, you never get it back. Childhood is fleeting. When it is in its formative stages, you get one chance.

You can also miss the chance to learn. Children teach you a lot more than you teach them. They give you a second chance to see the world for the first time through their eyes. And you will be astounded what you miss in the clutter of life. Hold onto those times while you can. As the nun sang in *The Sound of Music*, you can't keep a wave upon the sand. And you look kinda ridiculous trying.

In the workforce, always act like you are 35

When you are young in the workplace, don't act as a novice. If you are smart and competent, step up and do whatever you are capable of doing in a mature way. Similarly, when you are an older worker, don't act like it. Approach your day with youthful energy. To quote a famous Frank Sinatra song: "You're 35 and it's a very good year".

Management is about people, not things

It is easy to fall into the trap of believing that all people are equal, behave the same every day and have a generic capacity to perform. Humans are simply not made like that. The late business guru Jack Welch said the workforce consisted of 20 per cent of people who are high performers, 10 per cent who you should get rid of and 70 per cent who do okay. The real problem is the 70 per cent. Most managers want everyone in the 20 per cent. We need to be careful not to believe that the 70 per cent are underperformers. Sometimes we need to celebrate the competence of the masses not just the superpowers of the elite. As managers, we are not managing things, we are empowering people and making the best use of whatever it is they bring to the table.

Genuinely listen to others

It is easy to fall into the trap of thinking we have all the answers as individuals. We don't. As a group we are far more powerful. We need to learn to genuinely collaborate and really listen to the opinions of others. And we need to ask our own people first. So many managers and firms fall into the trap of seeking answers externally and then trying to implement the changes without authentic input from tried-and-true employees. In almost every case, our own people already know the answers. We need to avoid letting familiarity blind us to the talent sitting around us.

Never work for horrible bosses

Life is way too short to tolerate really bad bosses. If you find yourself working for one start looking for a new job. Immediately. Then sack the bad boss. By leaving.

Recognise that staff are people with finite emotional capacity

It is clear to me now that humans have a finite emotional capacity. If there is something challenging happening in their personal lives, they have limited capacity left to deal with issues at work. In nearly 100 per cent of cases I have dealt with of people suddenly under-performing at work, it has nothing to do with work. When good people have problems, managers and companies need to carry them. This should be a personal mission. If we learn to carry people when they most need it, we become a stronger community and we empower people in ways that we probably can't imagine when we are young. A re-invigorated previously broken employee is a corporation's most powerful force. They become a slightly better version of themselves.

Do not just network with people your own age

Beware the whiz kid syndrome. Smart, young people have a habit of forming communities of other smart young people and feeding off each other's energy. In the older world they are seen as "bright young things" who give confidence that the future is in good hands. Argghhhh! How many times have you heard that? Youth enclaves can actually be restrictive. Smart 20-somethings should make sure they network with older people too. In fact, their networking should be about meeting useful mentors and career champions who can open doors and fast track careers. Similarly, older, successful people should not just sit in musty clubs talking about the 1970s. They should be proactively seeking out smart, young people who can shake them out of their comfort zone and open their eyes to new ideas.

Celebrate cultural differences in the workplace

One of the big mistakes we make in my home country of Australia is failing to adequately recognise the value of overseas experience and people from a variety of cultures. Diversity brings a richness to our workplaces that benefits all of us. Overseas experience is real experience. We should take every opportunity to inject new thinking into our workplaces. It is where the magic begins.

Take the time to understand what your business does

I love the story of President John F Kennedy's visit to NASA during which he asked a cleaner what his job was. The cleaner replied that he sent rockets to the moon. All of us should feel part of what our organisations actually do. We should take the time to be part of the big picture and always feel connected with the true objectives of our workplace. Don't wait for someone to tell you or lament that internal communication is poor. Find out for yourself.

Do not put off working in another country

Geography is becoming less relevant. We are all citizens of the world. President Obama made the point during a speech in Australia during the 2014 G20 meeting that the world was becoming smaller and even the Pacific Ocean was now just a lake. If you get the chance to work overseas, and you aspire to do that, take it. There is never a right time. And we always regret the things we do not do far more than the things we do.

Work in an office where you have friends

You will spend a lot of time at work. You should work with people you like. I used to be a bit sceptical about a question in employment engagement surveys asking people if they had a "best friend" at work. I realise now that work is much better if you are among friends. The happiest people are those who do things they are passionate about with people they really like. Further to that, if you find you have taken on a job you hate, ditch it quickly. Your career can survive a few well-intentioned detours and mistaken pathways.

Never sacrifice personal ethics for a work reason

Crucial to workplace happiness is value alignment. If you work somewhere that compromises your personal ethics and values, get out of there as quickly as you can. Good people will be unnerved by things that don't feel right. If it doesn't feel right, it probably isn't. Bad things only manifest when good people don't take a stand.

Recognise that failure is learning

As bizarre as it might sound, failing is not failure. Researchers recognise that failure is just part of a process to eliminate unsuccessful options. To somewhat misquote Woody from the *Toy Story* movie, when we make a few mistakes, we are not failing, just falling – with style. Even fairy-tale princesses recognise that you need to kiss a lot of toads before you find a handsome prince. Thomas Edison articulated this best: "I have not failed. I have just found 10,000 ways that don't work." If we fear failure, we tend to take a minimalist approach to our jobs and the opportunities around us. Take some risks. Sometimes failing spectacularly is the best evidence that we are alive, human and serious about aspiring to the extraordinary. There is no value in being ordinary when you have the capacity to be remarkable.

Now, to get started on that time machine…

2. More career advice I wish I had earlier

Since writing the original *Career Advice I Wish I Had at 25* article I have kept building the list. Here are a few more things I would tell my younger self:

The only real expert on your life is you

The world is full of people who will have an opinion on your life. Social media has given all of them a voice. The reality is there is only one true expert on your life – you. Ultimately you must be true to yourself, find your own path and set your own values. So many people waste so many of their years living the life that is expected of them rather than the life they choose for themselves. Most ultimately regret it. As John Lennon said: "There ain't no guru who can see through your eyes".

You are the CEO of your career

I have a lot of conversations with people who lament that they are not getting ahead with their careers. In most cases they are waiting for something to happen.

For a long time, I was the same. I thought if I sat at my desk and worked hard, everything that I wanted to do would probably just happen one day. Like magic. Unfortunately, it doesn't work like that.

As soon as I became proactive, sought out business mentors and told the right people what I wanted to do, things happened quickly. You can't wait for magic. Ultimately you are the only person waking up in the morning thinking specifically about your life and career. You need to manage it and chase down what you want. You are the CEO of your life. You make the calls.

You have two parallel careers

Everyone has their official career (what they do for a living) and their other career. The other career is what you do in your unofficial corporate space.

This might include taking on an executive role in a networking or advocacy group, volunteering on a not-for-profit board, or even being the person who organises a gathering of contacts. This can be as important as what you do in the office. In particular, it can be a way to gain experience in a position of responsibility before your formal career reaches that point.

As a kid, I always found it interesting that the people who ran the Lions Clubs, Apex, Scouts etc quite often were not in management (or even senior) roles in their day jobs. Much of their sense of prestige and pride came from the success they felt from their unofficial career.

It is okay to say no

Plenty of books have been written around saying no. Many successful people quote the ability to say no as one of the keys to their success. There is something in this. Saying no all the time won't get you anywhere but, if you don't take charge of our own priorities, somebody else will. When this happens you inevitably burn a lot of time doing things that are of low value.

Being polite and accommodating can be a very positive trait. Being too polite and accommodating can waste a lot of your life and career. It can also stretch you so thin that you become less effective and successful.

Sometimes doing nothing is the best plan

In contemporary society, there is constant pressure to "do something". As a result, every time something happens, we end up with more and more legislation and regulations to try to keep everybody happy. This develops an expectation that other people, particularly people in authority, are responsible for solving all our problems.

In corporate world, an enormous amount of management time is spent "doing something" about every issue that gets raised by everybody. It takes many years to realise that quite a few issues work through and resolve without the need for a central process or symbolic action. This is certainly not always the case, but it pays to pause and question whether we really need to do something. There are plenty of times when doing something just makes things worse or more complicated.

Sometimes doing nothing (or at least delaying a response) can be the best tactic. Time can heal and sometimes enduring improvement comes from working through issues at the source rather than imposing a solution. The best solutions tend to be the ones we come up with ourselves.

The past is gone. Learn from it and move on.

Lament is a very common emotion. Most of us beat ourselves up over things we didn't do or poor decisions we made. If only we had bought the right shares or invested in the right real estate. If only we had studied a different degree.

The truth is the past is gone. You cannot go back. You can't rewrite it. It is useful to learn from history but there is no upside in wasting a single moment lamenting it. What you can do is control the present and plan the future. There is no right time to start anything and, as long as you draw breath, it is never too late to start something.

Marvel comic legend Stan Lee was nearly 40 when he wrote his first comic. Julia Child wrote her first cookbook at 50, Colonel Sanders franchised KFC at age 62. Warren Buffett created nearly all of his wealth after he turned 50. There are no use-by dates on people. The future is still yours. It is quite a gift.

Roll with it

It is easy to spend a lot of time fighting the tide and resisting the demands of life. But you can't fight life. If you do it is exhausting. You need to roll with it.

Countless words have been written about finding work-life balance. What you really need is life balance. In many contemporary professional jobs, it is really hard to draw a solid line between paid work and the rest of your life. Your work and personal phones are usually the same device. There are events, there are things to be read, often your best friends are people you work with.

It is okay to have a blurred line as long as you still have the right amount of rest, sleep, leisure and time for family and friends. It is far more productive to ask if you are living the life you desire than to ask if you have the right work-life balance. Life balance and flexibility seem like more appropriate contemporary aspirations. You need to find the flow and ride it.

Do not treat busyness as a virtue

The character George Costanza in the *Seinfeld* sitcom managed to successfully hold down a job by doing nothing but looking busy and frazzled all the time. The word busy is one of the most overused in our language. Everyone is busy. All the time. And you have no extra hours you can add to the day. By definition you are busy doing something all the time. It just comes down to what mindset you bring to that. Generally, if we convince ourselves we are busy we go into a negative mindset. However, organising priorities around the time we have can feel really good. In a similar vein, so-called "face time" or staying at work longer than you need to is rather ludicrous (yes, I've done it too). Everyone I know who has done this has regretted it later in life. Your time is worth fighting for. (More on this in Section 3).

Speak up

Some of the smartest people with the best ideas never say anything at meetings. You need to remember that you are the expert at whatever job you are doing. Meetings can be intimidating but there is seldom a downside to giving a respectful, well-considered opinion on something you know about. The corporate world is full of stories of people who gave a frank and respectful opinion at a meeting and immediately elevated their career status as a result, sometimes spectacularly. Your opinion matters and people will respect you for giving it.

Promote yourself (carefully and humbly)

There is an old phrase that talks about people "hiding their light under a bushel" (in Australia a bushel is a name for a wooden crate). It is a neat way of describing the many people who have held back their careers by never putting their hands up for a different, better or more senior job or articulating their value. As a result, no one imagines them into a higher job, and they are always overlooked. Boasting and arrogance are a bad look. On the flipside, many of us are humble by nature and believe opportunities will just come along if we sit and wait for them. If you are ambitious, people need to know. This can be as simple as asking to act in a higher role when someone is on leave, or going to a leader in the organisation and letting them know that you want to be considered for other things. Better still, go and ask what it would take for you to get ahead. That way someone else has a stake in your success.

Gain genuine extra expertise in multiple things

In the past you could get away with having a single deep qualification and a few shallow skills. In the new economy, this is not enough. You need to be seen as a real expert in several things to keep an edge and you need to have a mindset of constant reinvention to avoid being left behind.

A lot of people achieve the extra expertise by seeking leadership roles in organisations or professional associations outside of work. It is well documented that the most successful scientists in history had very high-level skills (music, art, sport etc.) outside of science.

We all need to take charge of our own careers to prevent us being left behind by the forces of change. And you cannot rely on "the system" to secure your future.

Target people and companies you want to work for rather than just apply for jobs

It can be a fairly sobering experience to constantly check job advertisements and then apply for jobs. You are usually up against hundreds of people and some highly programmed HR "bot" might bounce you out of contention before a human even looks at your application.

Careers are a long-term game. It is better to research companies with a culture and activities that appeal to you and proactively seek a relationship with these companies. A lot of really great jobs are never advertised. I've seen many examples of people who seek out companies they like, find mentors there and just morph into the organisation. Some companies even create jobs for them.

Value yourself and your life enough to ask

Too many people too quickly let themselves become victims. They lament that they miss something because they have to work, but they don't actually ask if they can have time off to do it. They lament that they don't have enough holidays but don't ask about unpaid leave or leave in advance. There is something that bugs them at work every day, but they never ask anybody if it can be fixed. They get overlooked for every opportunity, but they never ask for opportunities.

You really need to value yourself enough to ask. The answer will sometimes be no but quite often it will be yes. It never hurts to ask. What do you have to lose?

Give the gift of trust

Trust is one of the most valuable gifts you can give. If you trust an employee or a colleague to do something without looking over their shoulder or trying to micro-manage them, they tend to take that seriously and work very hard to deliver. Great leaders trust their people. They give broad direction but empower their people to find the best way to deliver the outcomes. Sadly, we have started to lose our trust in many of the things we grew up to value. We can only restore it when we all take the trust we are given seriously. And we all give trust in return.

Be kind

We live in a world that we have allowed to become infested with trolls and toxin, and a society where too many people seem to be looking for something to get outraged about. I don't think humans do well in that type of world. They harbour secret stresses and too easily get swept up in the lynch mob mentality and start exhibiting behaviours at odds with their values.

There is always the option to be kind. We can decide to look out for people who just need a friendly word to get them through. We can respect and value someone's opinion (even if we disagree with it) instead of attacking them. We have the option of giving people the benefit of the doubt a bit more and recognising that someone might just be having a bad day when they stuff up. People get tired. They are human. Sometimes they need a second chance.

It costs nothing to be kind but it has the power to light up the darkest corners of our bleakest days.

Have a growth mentality rather than a downsizing mentality

In a contemporary, constantly disrupting economy, the language of downsizing can become all pervasive in a workplace. CEOs are never game to rule out job cuts (who can predict it?) and there seems like a constant threat hanging over every workplace. This creates a climate of fear that is not conducive to audacious thinking and risk taking.

In this climate it can be easy to forget that growth is possible in any economy and the best way to stifle growth is to talk yourself out of it. Some businesses are failing purely because they have lost their confidence. Businesses maintain success through confidence and a growth plan that everybody believes in.

In the 21st Century business environment, we have to cut and expand simultaneously to evolve organisations at sufficient speed to stay competitive. Previously we tended to be doing one or the other, depending on the economic cycle. But, for the sake of the workforce psyche, the overarching message needs to be one of growth. And no company has ever just cut its way to growth. We all need a growth plan we believe in. Otherwise, we might as well shut the doors and go home.

SECTION 2

Reimagining your career

"The beginning is always today."
- **Mary Shelley** (English novelist)

It is easy to feel like you are in a rut. This is reinforced by the nature of day-to-day living. We go to bed, we get up, we eat, we work, we squeeze a few things in between and then we do it all again. The endless cycle of days tends to work against genuinely disrupting ourselves.

This section takes a practical look at how you can reboot your career at any time just by deciding to do it. And there is always a good time to start. Now.

1. It is never too late to reboot

I have always loved this quote: "It is never too late to be what you might have been." The line is generally attributed to 1800s author George Eliot (aka Mary Ann Evans). Whoever said it, those few words always make me stop and think.

The quote came back to me a few years ago when I was reading the book *Jumping Ship* by the then Goodstart Early Learning chairman and Social Ventures Australian founding CEO Michael Traill.

The book chronicles Michael's journey from the "millionaire's factory" of Macquarie Bank to a new life pioneering social enterprise and new approaches to not-for-profit business. In the early chapters of his book Michael relates the story of a forum conducted with a group of investment bankers and social entrepreneurs by renowned Scottish leadership thinker Professor Norman Drummond.

During the day, Professor Drummond, an author, executive coach, social entrepreneur and former BBC Governor, posed three simple questions to the assembled group:

- Who are you?
- Why are you living and working the way you currently are?
- What might you yet become and do with the rest of your life?

As Michael describes it, when the questions really began to sink in, "a bit of magic" started to happen.

He writes: "It was well captured by a colleague who said, 'Mate, I don't know where you got this guy from but I'm having conversations that I haven't had since I drank too much at uni. And it actually feels pretty good!"

"Curiously, but revealingly...some were writing surreptitiously, as though needing to write the questions down was a sign of weakness, or they felt some embarrassment at acknowledging their significance."

When you reflect on this, it really is so easy to look at life as some sort of sliding scale where "my day" (as in "back in my day") is in the past – where you reach some point when you are done and then you just flatline and wait around for retirement or fade to invisibility through a creeping irrelevance.

Someone wrote to me recently who talked about reaching the age of 39 and feeling like he had started to "stand still". The trouble, of course, with standing still is that the world keeps moving around you. You can so easily be left behind. The further behind you get, the harder you have to run to get back in the race.

Sometimes you get so caught up in the routine of relentless 24-hour cycles you keep your existence on autopilot and lose your sense of what you really want from life. Or you retire too early and revolve your life around watching soap operas and calling talkback radio because nobody gets it.

The reality is that, when you get past the heady younger years, there is every chance that you feel no different inside your head than you did at 30. Your body still works fine, you have lots of useful life and work experience and you can reinvent yourself whenever you want – If you choose.

Too many people settle, make up excuses to give up on

their dreams and start to convince themselves they are too old to do things when their lives should just be warming up.

It really is challenging to ask who you really are. It is confronting to question yourself honestly about why you live and work the way you do. But it is genuinely empowering to really ask what you might yet become if you disrupt yourself and stop letting your bike be pulled along in the slipstream of the pack.

As actor Christopher Walken so eloquently puts it, it is time to "say the truth that you're carrying in your heart like hidden treasure".

Most of the barriers to change are self-constructed. Now is always the best time to make positive change. And I can guarantee you, no matter who you are, how old you are and what you do, if you are reading this there is a good chance you still have the option to be what you might have been.

2. Getting your groove back at work

I remember reading a few years ago that, up until about the 1980s, most large US firms had the goal of creating jobs as part of their corporate visions. Then this aim quietly fell out. Business became more about earning money and giving adequate returns to stakeholders. Creating jobs was somebody else's problem. Times were tough. Business needed to cut and outsource. It was every man for himself.

In fact, few corporate "visions" over some decades focussed on improving the world and the lives of others. There were some very notable exceptions but, by and large, somewhere along the way we convinced ourselves that the heart of a business was just about making money. This was probably a big mistake. Successful business is actually about value-adding people's lives and providing a valuable service that they need. Making money is generally the consequence of that.

Sadly, in this corporate environment that has become so pragmatic and results-focussed, it is easy for employees to start to feel disconnected from outcomes and a little soulless in their jobs. When this happens, people tend to become job fickle, seeking variety as a cheap substitute for the passion they crave.

Thankfully, we have now entered an era where purpose, in its broadest sense, is back at the heart of many companies. In fact, emerging generations often put it at the top of the list when they are making decisions on where they want to work. Working just for the sake of money is taking a back seat to contributing to the planet and society more broadly.

US President Theodore Roosevelt believed that the best prize life had to offer was the chance to work hard at something worth doing. I'm not sure it is the "best prize," but I expect most of us would put it in the top five.

Over the course of a lifetime, the average person will spend more than 80,000 hours at work and a fair bit of the rest of their lives asleep. In that context, we should all be striving to extract as much positive energy as possible out of our workday. Equally, we should ensure that each precious day has a moment or two that lodges in our long-term memory and leaves an imprint on the world that will endure and nourish the lives of others.

So, how do we avoid that feeling of job emptiness? Here are a few thoughts.

Stay connected to what you really do

It is so easy to fall into the trap of believing your job is just about meeting your targets and achieving your corporate Key Performance Indicators (KPIs). It isn't. That is merely how we keep score. Your job is actually about providing a service or product that helps others to be more successful or fulfilled in their business, work or personal lives. If you concentrate on that, and do it well, the job will be more rewarding and the targets and KPIs will generally just look after themselves.

Connect emotionally, not just logically

I have done a lot of brand development work with many different organisations. The biggest trap most of them fall into is going straight for logical and practical messages around their brands and getting caught up in product attributes without delving deep enough into the benefits of those attributes.

In reality, the logical part of our brain is small compared to the powerful emotional centre. And emotion tends to feed our long-term memories and response structures. In this mix, logic can battle for attention.

The truly great brands do not rely on logic. They stand for something; they share values with their customers, and they make money as a consequence of doing what they do very well. Making money is not core to their purpose or the reason they exist..

Understanding the emotional benefits of what you do can give you a strong sense of purpose and help make your job more satisfying. Try asking yourself how your role helps improve the world. You can make a real difference to the people you interact with each day, and great companies who connect deeply with customers tend to be the most successful.

Give the gift of time

The most precious gift any of us have is our time. It is, by definition, finite. When people give us their time, for any purpose, we should really value that and never waste it. Similarly, sometimes people just need a bit of our time to make their day better. If you give some of it to somebody who needs it, just because you can, you will realise later that your day was better for it. If everyone does it, we all benefit.

Take the time to praise someone

A lot of people lament that they work really hard and never get any positive feedback. Often the same people do not give positive feedback. If everybody made an effort just to praise someone who really deserved it, this could be enough to put a spring in their step and make them feel valued. Workforces in this mode are not only more productive, they create better working environments every day of the year.

Create something

For most people, creating something is more satisfying than just processing stuff. Yet how often do we just get caught up in processing what is there rather than looking for better ways and better things? A good start would be to stop treating the term "innovation" as some sort of exotic animal bred by new-age people with laisse-faire hairstyles. Innovation is a state of mind and a way to work, not a "thing" that needs its own department and bureaucratic process.

Find out something new

We never stop learning but we can easily stop actively growing our knowledge and start outsourcing our brains to Google. There are few things more powerful and satisfying than learning a new fact that enriches your work, life or conversation. This can be as simple as proactively following up something that came up during the day and you didn't know about before. Days that you finish feeling like you have genuinely learnt something never feel like empty days.

Craft a memory

Most humans live tens of thousands of days but remember very few of them. At least once or twice a week we should do memorable things that engrave hard into our long-term memories. Life shouldn't be blah. We should seek out people, activities, places and experiences that leave an indelible mark in our minds and a place holder that can feed future understanding and insights.

Give somebody a break, just because you can

Most days we have a choice between making somebody's day miserable or okay. We can complain or not complain. We can point out a fault or we can just let it pass. We can argue vehemently against someone, or not. We can be constructive, or destructive. Sometimes the waitress is just having a bad day or the taxi driver took a wrong turn by mistake. We are all human but we regularly convince ourselves that we have to bring somebody to task because it is the right thing to do. Often it isn't.

It can be better for the world in general, and the way we feel, if the default is to give people the benefit of the doubt, at least in the first instance. We shouldn't ignore serial shoddiness but if our inclination is always to find fault, that behaviour can infect us all with a toxin. We can easily spend our lives waiting for everyone to stuff up so we can have a smug "got you" moment. A genuine mistake forgiven is a real gift towards somebody else's confidence and feelings of self-worth. Great communities primarily support each other, not drag each other down.

Be in the now, not a hypothetical future

It is hard to have a working day with meaning if you are not actually in it. Some people experience every day wishing it was over. Before long you are wishing your week away to get to the weekend, wishing your months away to get to Christmas or a holiday and wishing your years away to get to retirement. Then you eventually die, but not before regretting all the things you didn't do on all those days you had. Days only have meaning if you are in them and squeezing every bit of opportunity for engagement, creativity, meeting new people and learning new things. Anything less is just a waste of a perfectly good day.

Learn from someone you do not know well

This is a surprisingly enriching thing to do. Author and happiness researcher Shawn Achor says we should smile at anyone who comes within three metres of us and say hello to anyone who comes within 1.5 metres. This feels strange initially but produces an astonishing number of genuine smiles. Travelling in a lift or waiting in a queue is a great opportunity to meet a new person and enjoy a 30-second conversation with them. This always feels like a value-add to life. I fear social media has left us starved of face-to-face conversation. When we go out of our way to have an unexpected conversation it seems to activate something in the back of the mind that has been waiting patiently for a call. It is called socialisation and humans were constructed to do it, even shy humans.

Make some progress on a long-term plan

Workplaces are so busy that, without a proactive plan, we may never get to the long-term planning that matters. This includes fundamental changes to structures, writing complex strategy, creating important policy documents, looking beyond the next six months or researching best practice in the industry. We ignore these things because we know they take a lot of time and we can't find big blocks of time in our weeks.

If you follow the adage that you should eat an elephant one bite at a time, the progress comes. If you break the big stuff into chunks and set aside enough time to do the chunks, you fairly quickly get there on the big stuff. And it just feels good to make progress on something fundamental.

Make sure you have something to look forward to

It is vital for humans to have something to look forward to. The look-forward-to thing is really important in a work context. When you come back from a Christmas break, you should really plan and book your next holiday. That way, when you have bad days, you can just write them off as a stumble on the road to the next great thing. And nothing seems insurmountable when you know you can walk away from it for a while and you can count down the days to when something exciting will happen.

This can also occur on a smaller scale. Putting something you really enjoy in your diary every week means you always have a highlight point to anchor your week. This simple thing has a remarkable ability to dull off the bad days.

Reconnect with former colleagues

People really appreciate you making the effort, but it also helps to keep what author and speaker Richard Koch describes as "weak ties", alive. Too often we only get in touch with former colleagues when we want something. Contact is far more powerful when it is done just for the sake of it.

Make contact with someone you admire

Many years ago I met a boy whose hobby was writing to famous people. Remarkably a huge proportion of them wrote back. His collection of letters from world leaders and celebrities was astounding.

We all have people who we follow on blog sites or admire for various reasons. The digital world allows us to make contact with pretty much anybody. It is empowering to write to someone who has helped enrich your life or your understanding of something. It doesn't even matter if they don't return the contact. Making the effort to thank them or comment on their work is a reward in itself.

And sometimes digital is not the answer anyway. Try sending someone a good, old-fashioned letter. They are a very powerful form of communication. These days I tend to keep every personal letter or card sent to me through the post. They are special and I really appreciate that type of effort.

Concentrate on the things that unite us

As you get older you begin to realise that we really are, as Australian singer/songwriter Ben Lee sang, all in this together. When you really get to know people from different countries, races, religions and backgrounds you quickly realise that we mostly have the same aspirations, the same fears, the same hopes, the same insecurities, the same base moralities, the same desire to love and be loved and the same yearnings for a better and safer world. We even laugh at the same things. And a smile has the same positive impact across all cultures.

If the human race just prioritised the things that unite rather than divide us, the world would improve overnight. This can begin in the workplace where so many of us spend so much of our time. When we concentrate on people rather than things and work towards pursuits with genuine meaning rather than empty outcomes, we release endorphins rather than stress chemicals.

There are many things out of our control but also plenty of things that we totally control. Small changes can quickly conglomerate into megatrends. Every day we have a choice of going through the motions or creating something compelling and meaningful.

3. Making better use of your time

In a practical sense, there is a lot you can do in your working life to attract a better return on your investment in time.

Here are a few that work for me.

Spend time at your desk preparing for the day before it officially starts

Days always seem to produce better results when you start at least half an hour before you have to and do some things that are not mandatory for your job. This is a great time to get up to date with news from around the world, read an article from someone you admire, read something inspirational you filed away in the past or check out what events are happening on the weekend. When I do this, I always feel like I have stolen back some time for living and I feel far more intellectually nourished at the end of the week.

Deal with emails in a block at the end of the day

Most of us are easily distracted. You get started on something important and then an email comes in. So you answer it. Then you go back to the something important. And another email comes in. And you answer it. Before you know it several hours have passed, you have answered a whole lot of non-urgent emails and the important task is half done or feeling disjointed and unsatisfactory. Most emails can wait. And you can generally deal with a day's worth of email at the end of the day far more efficiently than jumping every time something comes into the inbox.

Do not overcrowd your to-do list

Most people have up to 20 things on their to-do lists and end every day with a sense of failure. If you have meetings and other commitments, there is not enough time for 20 things. Most of us get about three things done. Be realistic and just do those. The rest will need to be delayed or delegated. Set yourself up for success rather than failure and get real about how much you can do in a day.

Do not think that long hours are expected of you

In most workplaces, there is a sense of aura and respect for those who are first in and last out. They usually get bonuses and have a reputation for a strong work ethic and dedication. But, unless your job is fantastic, it is not a great way to live. And sometimes you get addicted to the reputation (see burnout chapter in Section 5). If you suddenly decide just to work less hours, it is astounding how you can find ways to get everything done in that time. People who expect to work 12-hour days tend to unconsciously spread their work over that number of hours. Others seem to get the same amount done in eight.

In print newspapers, for example, you have to hit the button on an edition at the same time every day regardless of whether it is a quiet news day or planes have flown into the twin towers. People in that industry have a remarkable ability to find ways to achieve a lot in a short period of time when it is a priority, or there is no choice. I'm yet to see any career hampered by working fewer hours but still achieving the expected results.

Have a day a week when you do not do meetings

Meetings can suck the life out of your day. In an Outlook world, all meetings tend to be blocked out in half-hour or one-hour blocks. The concept of "no meeting Friday" is very powerful. It is a great way to end the week with some time to get work done and to go to the weekend without that awful sense of unfinished business that can mess with your relaxation mindset. "No meeting Friday" only works if you just knock back meeting requests no matter who they come from. Easier said than done. But doable. And incredibly liberating.

Diarise time to do work

If you only use your diary for meetings, you may struggle to get everything done that you need to do. It is actually far more important to diarise time for actual work. The trick is to block out the time in your diary to complete a task, agree with yourself that you will finish the task during that time, ignore any distractions and make sure you have accurately judged how much time is needed for the task. This process is incredibly satisfying and also gives you a sense that you are in control of your week, and you don't have to "find time" to complete something important. Don't find time – allocate time.

Spend at least 30 minutes a day just thinking

Our brains are at their best without "noise" and bombardment. A bit of time spent thinking, and getting some sunshine, can get your brain into a different dimension and better equipped to find innovative answers to compelling issues. We sometimes kid ourselves that we need to be working intensely all the time to be effective. Sometimes what we really need is some clear air. A half hour spent thinking can be more effective than two hours battling an issue through clutter, noise and pressure.

4. Money – how much do you really need?

When I was about 10 years old, I bought an issue of *Cracked* magazine from a second-hand bookstore in my hometown. One of the sections was a satirical take on famous words of wisdom. The one I remember is: "Money can't buy happiness, but it can make misery a lot more fun."

The idea that money cannot buy happiness has been part of the cultural landscape for a long time. It is borne out by countless pieces of research.

Of course, like most things in life, it is not that simple.

Since humans in the Western world moved away from a subsistence existence, the amount of money we have has become a large driver of the type of life we lead. It dictates where we live, what we drive, how often we can eat out and attend entertainment events, where our children go to school, the quality of our medical care and the type and frequency of our holidays.

Financial security can be a big factor in the stability and harmony of our relationships. The motive to increase wealth is considered a major driver of activity in a capitalist economy and a big incentive for people to perform well at work or start businesses.

It is true that money alone does not provide happiness and plenty of people with very little money are very happy.

On the other hand, for most of us, we are kidding ourselves if we think we would be content to be poor. For every individual there is a balance point where the income and contentment equation is in equilibrium.

A few years ago, I interviewed one of Australia's richest men and asked him about his net worth. He was often referred to as a billionaire but more recently there had been reports that he was really "only" worth a few hundred million.

He told me: "Once you've got five or 10 million dollars your lifestyle remains the same if you've got $1 billion or $5 billion." He lived a fairly lavish lifestyle but whether he was worth $200 million or $2 billion didn't make any real difference and he didn't personally keep track of his net worth.

The late Australian media magnate Kerry Packer was once asked why he gambled such huge amounts at the casino. He said to be a true gambler, the money you put on the table had to hurt if you lost it. And Mr Packer was so wealthy he had to bet a lot before it hurt.

It is all relative. Most of us will never be worth $10 million and certainly not have the wealth of Kerry Packer but most of us also do not need that much to support our lifestyles and find our contentment equilibrium.

Personally, I have never desired great wealth. The test for me is that I want:

- A comfortable house within 30 minutes of where I work
- The ability to cover bills and expenses without any stress
- A serviceable car (I have no status need around this)
- The ability to eat out and attend concerts on a reasonably regular basis without having to think about it too much
- The ability to have a domestic holiday once a year and an overseas holiday at least every 2-3 years

This equilibrium requires me to earn a reasonably high salary. Beyond that there is a declining marginal return on anything extra I earn.

The income equilibrium point is a crucial conversation we all need to have with ourselves, and our significant others, when making career decisions.

Some people make very bad decisions purely on the basis of money. Many people get caught working long hours in grinding jobs because they get addicted to the wealth that comes from that and realise too late that they have squandered valuable time and the things that really matter.

Some people are obsessed with the adage of "keeping up with the Jones's". They feel the need to be seen to be successful relative to other people and to display trappings of wealth. Often, they take on large debt just to achieve that. I have never met anyone who does this who seems genuinely happy. The whole process seems to drain and traumatise them.

Of course, there are plenty of people who just like nice things, and there is nothing wrong with that.

At the other end of the scale, I have worked with plenty of unhappy people who took a job at a lower level than a previous role and resented it from day one. Realistically, you cannot blame your employer if you accept a job at a salary level you were not happy with.

Employers and recruiters will generally ask about your "salary expectations" when you are in a job change process. That is a perfectly reasonable thing to ask.

When it happens, you need to ask yourself a more complex question related to your income, lifestyle and job satisfaction equilibrium.

If the job pays less than your salary expectations does it make up for it in other ways – such as job satisfaction, a sense of purpose or being in your element?

If you take a lower salary will you resent it later? What is important to your lifestyle, and will you still be able to fund it if you do that job?

How much money do you really need?

That final question is what it all comes down to. There are many lottery winners on the record saying that the windfall ruined their lives. Almost everyone who gets a pay rise or a better paying job immediately scales up the cost of their lifestyle and the extra income just normalises into their budgets.

There is no evidence that wealth per se is synonymous with happiness and authentic quality of life. Non-material things are clearly more enriching for the human soul.

Ultimately you just need to be true to yourself. And live your own life, not one of constant comparison with somebody else. You can't take it with you. And if you are going to be miserable in life, you might as well have some fun doing it.

5. Why certain people get ahead

At 27 years of age, I was first flung into a senior management job requiring supervision of large numbers of people and the hiring of staff.

At the time I was a lot younger than many of the people I was supervising. So I took the advice of Mark Twain and exercised a combination of ignorance and confidence to bluff my way through. Some days I got away with it.

Since then, it has been fascinating to watch a generation of employees traversing the complex maze of career disruption, organisational commotion, economic fluctuations and promotion psychology. Some have fulfilled their ambitions, a handful of those very quickly. Others have flat-lined (many quite happily) while many more seem to have just disappeared into a back office somewhere, leaving scarcely a shadow or a footprint in the corporate or digital world.

When I consider which employees have fulfilled their ambitions, nearly all displayed some combination of these traits:

They bring solutions instead of just problems

In management you spend a lot of time dealing with problems that are brought to your attention. Very quickly you start to notice people who bring you problems that are already packaged with a potential solution. In fact, that trait is probably the key attribute of people who really get ahead in their careers.

They enjoy the job, but they enjoy something outside of work even more

Contrary to the popular myth, most successful people don't seem to be obsessed with their jobs. They find jobs that are fulfilling but generally they have an outside passion (sport, hobby, family etc) that really drives them. The combination of work success and an outside passion gives them a life comfort that seems to help them float up the corporate ladder with apparent ease. They can tolerate the tough workdays because their lives are balanced, and they don't worry unnecessarily about trivial problems.

They work long hours only when needed

This demonstrates their confidence in their value and abilities, but also the value they place on a holistic life. It is easy to fall into the habit of treating long, hard days as normal. The most successful people don't have this type of normal. They work smart and appropriately. These are the same group who tend to become successful CEOs because they have the confidence to rise above the noise and give themselves time to think and function properly.

German Second World War Commander General Field Marshal Erich von Manstein advised his country's army to leave the lazy, stupid soldiers alone because they would do no harm, put the hardworking intelligent soldiers into senior (but not too senior) positions, get rid of the hardworking, stupid soldiers because they would do damage and put the lazy, intelligent ones in charge. Some version of that tends to happen in many corporate settings.

They stay calm in all circumstances

No matter where you work, there will be a crisis from time to time. People who get ahead tend to be at their best in a crisis. They stay measured, they do not panic, and they use experience and good advice from others to make sound calls. This approach inspires confidence and helps to deal with issues without too much brain static or ill-directed adrenalin.

They learn to do effective presentations

Presentations are a big part of corporate life and the people who get ahead tend to make it their business to do these well. This does not come easily to some people, but I have seen many who are not natural presenters become very astute at it through sheer tenacity and practice.

The good ones also find an authentic presentation style. They do not try to be funny if that does not come naturally and they use great visuals if they need to mask nerves or take attention from themselves.

Renowned American newspaper publisher Joseph Pulitzer had some good advice on communicating with impact: "Put it before them briefly so they will read it, clearly so they will appreciate it, picturesquely so they will remember it and, above all, accurately so they will be guided by its light."

They nail each level before moving to the next

The best people tend to keep climbing the ladder, and often make it look effortless. This is generally because they work hard at being superb at their current job, then they outgrow it and morph naturally to the next level. Those who push too hard, too early seem to eventually get promoted one level beyond their readiness and this can put a taint on them and set their careers back years.

At the other end of the spectrum, some people wait too long to push for promotion and get stuck in a comfort zone. You need to get the balance right.

They tend to defend rather than attack people behind their backs

A former boss of mine was a stickler for "defending the absent". Few people are saintly enough to do this all the time, but I have found the really successful people I have worked with over the years tended to have this trait. By defending people who are not in the room they give those who are in the room confidence that they will also be defended. As a natural extension, the people who defend the absent tend to also get defended when they are not in the room. This is a great hedge against career damage and attacks that you can't see. It is also the right thing to do.

They make their ambition known so they are seen in that light

The people who get ahead tend to continuously position themselves as future leaders. Over the years I have known many people who had been doing the same job for 10 years or more and then divulged in a performance review that they were actually ambitious and wanted to be in senior management. Unfortunately, nobody had ever perceived them in that light and hence they could not be imagined into the next position.

Similarly, deputies to key roles often don't get promoted to the main role because they come to be seen as number-twos rather than leaders. I actually reached a stage in my career where I refused to take any job with "deputy" in the title. Whatever I was doing I wanted to be a real, autonomous job, not an offshoot of someone else's job.

They exercise as part of their routine

A large proportion of successful "self-made" people are physically fit as well as mentally fit. To sustain a long career and cope with stress, exercise tends to be vital. People with fit bodies tend to also have fit minds and the ability to cope with pressure and prolonged bombardment.

They are well informed

Most senior jobs require formal qualifications but the majority of the successful people I have worked with have broad knowledge beyond their specific vocational training. In fact, I think a lot of their success comes from understanding the broader context of where the world is at during any point in history and ensuring the organisation they are working for remains relevant to that context. They ride emerging waves rather than just getting dumped onto the beach.

They network well but don't "hyper-network"

People tend to marvel at those with the knack of "working the room." They talk in hushed tones about how they float around the party like social apparitions making contact with everyone and showing an uncanny ability to remember names. This tends to work for celebrities and politicians who get the return because people put a value on meeting them without the need to engage more deeply.

For most other people, successful networking means targeting specific people at a networking event, spending some quality time with them to form a "memory bond" and then arranging a tangible follow-up later to cement the contract. If you hyper-network a room, there is a danger of social malnutrition and having a pocketful of business cards from people you still would not recognise in a police line-up. The successful people seem to acquire meaningful contacts rather than autographs and business cards.

They think a step or two ahead

Great sportspeople have the gift of time. They seem to instinctively weigh up a situation quickly and have more time than anyone else to exercise a play. Successful corporate executives are often the same. They are wired with an ability to take a few steps back and assess a situation from a broader perspective. The real skill is less about understanding the now and more about anticipating how current action will influence what happens next.

They document things but not to a ridiculous level

Recording plans, outcomes and actions can be important to ensuring tasks are completed with necessary rigour and discipline. The old management adage says you can't manage what you can't see. But there is a balance. The successful operators know the right mix between recording information and death by documentation. They also refuse to leave meetings until there is an action plan.

They build relationships at all levels

We have always been warned to be good to people when we are on the way up because you may be reporting to them on the way down.

Basic courtesy and respect should be a given between any layer of employee in any organisation. However, I have observed over the years that the really successful people go out of their way to form genuine bonds with people at all levels.

This has a variety of advantages. For a start a lot of the real intelligence in an organisation does not sit in the top rung. Cleaners, executive assistants, finance people and a plethora of other positions see the company from unique vantage points and can provide valuable opinions and insights for ambitious employees. What's more, one of the great skills of a leader or senior manager is having the internal and external contacts and information to act on something quickly and proficiently. If they are well connected within the organisation, they can quickly summon intelligence and make quality decisions.

They connect with the most senior person

There is a big difference between a meaningful relationship with the most senior boss and stalking them. The smart operators, from early in their career, work out how to be on the senior management radar without crossing the over-eager/highly annoying line. Typically, they will pass on some useful business intelligence every so often, or pass on regards from someone who has mutually crossed their paths. They might also do something particularly thoughtful or helpful, with no requirement for praise or acknowledgement. These simple things put them into a leadership positioning long before they are commanding an army.

6. Secrets of people who snare great jobs

Some years ago, I was part of a group developing an idea for a television show that took viewers inside the selection process for jobs.

It was called *Job Hunter* and it was predicated on a notion that the employment selection process was one of our most intriguing social dances, dappled in emotion, mind games and an ill-formed, slightly awkward corporate version of flirtation.

The show did not get picked up. However, I have remained a little fixated on the complex elimination process that can start with hundreds of candidates and culminate with a single "survivor" who takes all the career spoils. The rest just walk away to regroup for the next challenge. The tribe has spoken. Only one winner is left on the island.

On a rough calculation, I have conducted or been on selection panels for about 800 interviews over the years across media, business, universities, not-for-profit, government and marketing. A large chunk of these were in the 1990s when I was one of a small team doing shortlisting of candidates for cadet journalism roles. Typically, we started with several hundred candidates considered worthy of interview and a handful were offered employment.

During this process we saw it all. During one interview I opened with "so how are you? (Incisive I know)" and the young woman just collapsed into tears. For the next 45 minutes she told me that her boyfriend had left her, her friends didn't like her, she failed at everything, and the dog was sick. She didn't get shortlisted, but we had a good chat and she left smiling, apparently relieved at unburdening herself. I suspect she now watches *Dr Phil*.

But people do get selected. We all look for different things but in my experience the ones who most regularly come out on top have unlocked a few mysteries. They are not always the smartest or even the most qualified. They just know some of these secrets:

They recognise that job hunting is a "courtship"

There is much more to getting a great job than writing a sharp cover letter and having a CV that sparkles. In fact, if you are just waiting for a job to be advertised and then joining the hordes who apply for it, you are already up against it.

Written applications are flat and can almost never convey the "it" factors that snare most jobs. As a result, many of the right people don't get interviews. No matter how talented and experienced the people short listing are, with written applications alone they are pretty much ticking boxes on desired qualification matches and applying a bit of gut instinct based on the style of the application.

The smart people are courting the job and the organisation well before they are in a process. The company already knows they are interested in working there and they have sought a couple of "blind dates" with key people. They send in updated CVs as they gain experience and they have sought to engage with the company through networking events and other opportunities. Many employers are required under their rules to enact a selection process. In a very large number of cases, they are already emotionally committed to a potential employee who has been wooing them for months. By the time others enter the process they have already been out flanked.

They are "in" the job before the interview ends

There are two types of interviews. The first type is very formal, with a whole lot of predictable questions and safe answers that go on for about an hour and end with polite handshakes and estimates of when the panel might get back to you. The estimates are generally wrong.

Then there are the "alpha zone" interviews. These ones start with a couple of questions and then move quickly into a different zone. The panel and the candidate stop doing the dance of the strangers and effectively start planning what is going to happen when the person starts. This is not contrived. The alpha zone just happens. Immediately the panel get a little burst of euphoric adrenalin, which is a great feeling, and the candidate deep down knows that they are in.

Sometimes this is just a result of pure synergy and compatibility. More often it is because the candidate has genuinely mastered the secret of preparation. Instead of doing some scant web research on the company and reading the job description, they have spoken to people on the ground, picked up the corporate nuances and spent days doing what they would do anyway when or if they got the job. In the interview it comes across as the stars aligning. In reality it is just smart groundwork.

The great former News Corp Australia CEO John Hartigan used to talk about PLUs and the need to employ them in the organisation. This stood for People Like Us. Most companies are looking for people like them (people who share their core values and aspirations). In any process there are usually plenty of people qualified for the role. The thing you most look for is fit for the organisation. Smart people demonstrate unequivocally that they are PLUs. If they aren't, they are smart enough to avoid the organisation anyway.

They know it is not about them

I hate to be the one to break the bad news, but companies don't employ you to advance your career. It is not about you; it is about them. Just over half of all job application letters I receive start with a line on why the candidate wants the job and why it would be good for their career.

That's lovely and good luck with that. But what a company wants to know is what you can do for them. When anyone is hiring, they are looking for someone who will make them more successful – they want the whole to be greater than the sum of the parts. All applications should start with that. Hit them in the eye with enthusiasm, ideas and an unwavering belief that, by adding you to the company, the value you bring will be beyond anything they ever imagined in the role.

And it is never about wanting "a" job or "this type of role". I have never hired anyone unless I was totally convinced they wanted "this" job with its unique attributes – the perfect person for their perfect role.

They work out how to break through "the wall"

Any human conversation or interaction starts with something akin to a glass wall between the participants. When people are naturally compatible the wall comes down quickly. Some people work together for 20 years and never break through it.

People who manage to break down the wall during an interview have a very strong record of getting hired. You can hope that through some alignment of the stars, the wall just comes down while you are in the interview room. But that will seldom happen unaided.

Smart candidates know long before the interview where potential cracks in the wall are hidden. They research the panellists and find out what they are interested in, they look for points of common interest or colleague intersection, they discover something about the organisation that is of vital interest, or they pull out something compelling and unexpected that creates an empathy connection.

The other secret, which applies also to giving engaging speeches to a new crowd, is to always be prepared to give something of yourself to the interviewers. Tell a story against yourself – admit a blooper from your first job or a previous interview. Not only does this break down the wall, it sends a strong message that everything else you say will also be honest. Honesty is still one of the most powerful connectors when you look for new staff.

They leave something substantial behind with no expectation of a return

I seldom see this, but it is really powerful. A handful of times I have seen candidates at an interview hand over a document with some well-considered thoughts on the organisation and some constructive ideas on business improvement. This comes out at the end rather than during the interview and it is just given as a gesture of thanks for being considered. In some cases, even when the candidate doesn't get the job, the panel continues to talk the person up to others purely off the basis of that gesture. I have also seen it directly result in the person getting a different job in the organisation down the track.

They know about the lift test

Don't be fooled into thinking the interview process starts in the interview room. It really starts from the first point of contact and often the pre-interview steps are the most vital. If I am personally interviewing someone for a vital role, I make a point of meeting them in reception and walking them to the relevant office or travelling in the lift (elevator) with them. At least 90 per cent of the time I know before I get to the interview room whether they are a contender. First impressions really do count.

They turn a weakness into their greatest strength

Sometimes you have restrictions, limitations and issues that you think might inhibit your chances of getting a role you really want. This could be childcare issues that require you to work part-time, gaps in your resume or a lack of formal qualifications that the job spec says are vital. Never let that hold you back. In fact, try to turn your biggest weaknesses into your greatest assets.

If you need to work part-time, don't apologise for it, just go in with a plan that works for the employer. Budgets are always tight. Convince them that you can be as effective as a full-time employee while working less days and costing less money. If it works for you, submit a plan for your weeks that includes some night sessions (after kids are in bed) doing strategy and reports that don't have any tangible connection to daylight hours.

Do not sweat that you do not tick every box. Frankly these days I hate hiring anyone who is 100 per cent qualified. When that happens you generally just get what they did down the road replicated in your office. Organisations can get stuck in a loop that way. In the contemporary workplace we need new thinking and disruption. I like to hire smart people with around 70% of the required qualifications. The magic and fresh ideas come from the way they fill the 30%.

As for formal qualifications, most interview panels are empowered to ignore those requirements for the right person. Who really remembers the stuff from formal training anyway? And, given the rate of economic disruption, you need to be learning in real time to truly be qualified today. The real skill is in knowing where to get the information you need and getting good at something by doing it.

You won't always be able to pull this off, but you have nothing to lose by backing yourself. Weaknesses can so easily become superpowers.

They do everything just a bit better than the others

Olympic athletes often talk about training with their competitors in mind, knowing that if they are not doing the extra lap, or pushing themselves a little harder, their competitors probably are. Job preparation can be a bit the same.

Quite often, after a selection process, you get calls from unsuccessful candidates seeking feedback on what they did wrong. Very often they did nothing wrong. Someone else just did more things right.

To go back to the example of short-listing for newspaper cadets, in all the hundreds of people who applied, only a tiny number submitted perfect applications. In this field that would entail – stories already in the media through sheer tenacity, evidence of an ability to write, shorthand and typing, a strong general knowledge, an ability to hold an argument on current issues and enough demonstrated intelligence to go toe to toe with every level of society.

If you really want the job, don't just go through the motions. Set a goal of being perfectly prepared. You can guarantee at least one or two others will be. How much do you really want the role?

They keep it real

I dread those horrible interviews in which, five minutes in, the candidates start talking like a public sector selection criteria document and use words that should be restricted to 15th century legal documents. So many candidates start to sound like politicians churning out spin.

Do not be a contrived version of yourself – just be yourself! If you are good there is no reason to spin. Look people in the eye and give an honest answer. And do not think you are fooling anyone when you don't have a good answer and you try to make something up. Experienced interviewers immediately see the panic in your eyes. Your head might as well double in size and go bright green. Just be honest and live with the consequences. You aren't hiding anything, and nobody is perfect.

During the cadet journalist interviews, the candidates tended to tell each other to make sure they read the front page of that day's paper because we would ask them to talk about the stories. Of course, that seemed a little dull so I would often ask them what was on page four. I didn't care less if they knew. I was only interested in how they answered. Most panicked initially, some just took a bad guess. The best answer I got was from a young woman who looked me straight in the eye, without a nanosecond of hesitation, and said: "I have absolutely no idea but if you hand me that paper I can let you know in 20 seconds." Great answer.

They understand the power of story telling

Marketing yourself as the best candidate for a job is no different from marketing a company. It entails the same four components – make an emotional connection, create a favourable brand perception, find innovative ways to convey your ideas and infiltrate the long-term memory by communicating through story telling.

Always keep in mind that, even though every part of a formal job selection process is grounded in logic, the decisions are often grounded in emotion. Most employers will happily hire someone who they think will be a great fit and contributor to the organisation even when somebody else has better qualifications on paper. The best way to make an emotional connection in the confines of an interview is to tell powerful stories that illustrate the point. The result is empathy and emotional enrichment that makes a candidate highly compelling.

7. Repackaging yourself for success

As far back as the 1960s, Bob Dylan reminded us that the times they are a-changin'. They were. They are. They always do.

The job market is no different. It evolves in real time as employers seek complex new skillsets that match the new era of multitasks, rapid-change technology and mega-complex reasoning.

I have noticed this trend all over the workplace landscape. I seldom see it recognised in resumes.

Today, your resume should not just be a list of university degrees, diplomas and certificates of various colours, flavours and quality. It should not be only a list of jobs you have had and the dot points from your various job descriptions.

It needs to be a beautifully packaged bundle of what you can do, somewhat unshackled from traditional education structures and old-hat ways of describing our jobs.

Taking a less shackled approach to packaging your qualifications can also often help your career move without years of study. While most employees are still fairly fixated on formal qualifications, employers are increasingly okay with proof of the right skills rather than traditional pieces of paper.

This is not to downplay the role of formal qualifications. They will always be important. The trick is to evolve your personal packaging at the speed you are learning and present a compelling mix of your formal and micro-credentialled skills.

I have seen a lot of resumes over the years. Most could benefit from asking these three questions before they are locked in:

What are your real skills?

This question requires you to take a broader context. I've met employers in the past who hire a lot of people who are returning to the workforce after raising children. Why? It's not because they have a long CV of formal qualifications and experience. It is because they have an incredible work ethic and are great at multitasking. They don't give you a certificate for that.

Newspaper journalists are another good example. There are far fewer jobs in the newspaper industry now than at any time in the past 50 years, even with the growth of digital sites. As a result, many journalists are trying to repackage themselves for different roles.

In doing this, there is not a lot of point in doing a resume that shows you are qualified to be a newspaper journalist. You need to debundle your skills for different needs.

In fact, journalists have very marketable skills, namely:

- The ability to assess and summarise information quickly
- The ability to write for different audiences
- The ability to find angles in information that makes it interesting
- The ability to organise information logically
- The ability to work very quickly at a high level of accuracy
- The ability to mix and be effective at all levels of an organisation

In a world where companies are taking control of their

own communication channels and change is happening very quickly, these skills are in very high demand.

Often the best people do not get jobs because they make the mistake of packaging themselves for their old jobs in the old world, rather than re-bundling their skills for new jobs in the contemporary world.

Are you matching your skills with things that are in demand?

To that point, you need to organise your skills around the audience, not your life's chronology. And do not be afraid to leave things off. You need to tightly tailor your CV and cover letters for the particular purpose, not squeeze everything you have ever done in your life into these poor, overworked documents.

Most lists of the most marketable skills in the new economy include things like emotional intelligence, adaptability, communication and social media skills, the ability to analyze, creativity, management of complex and intergenerational teams, teamwork and ability to handle complexity.

In all the resumes I see, almost none tease out these highly marketable skills.

What are the real-world examples? You might as well get in ahead of the interview.

In the context of marketable skills, the best way to demonstrate these is through examples. In almost every interview, the stock questions include asking you to give examples to demonstrate how you have handled particular things.

In my experience, only about half of interviewees come prepared for this. Some have very awkward long pauses. Many remember a good example a few minutes after the interview and send a follow-up email (not a showstopper but better to be able to answer on the spot). In my view, a good CV should have some sharp examples of why and how you have the skills that are valued by contemporary organisations. I would much rather read that than a work and life history that just lists the things you turned up for. Anyone can do that. Why are you special?

8. Building your personal brand

In the contemporary, ultra-connected digital world we all have a personal brand, whether we want one or not. The way we position ourselves can have a big impact on careers, opportunities, and our ability to influence the change we want to see in the world. In fact, thousands of people are now building whole careers purely on creating personal brands and becoming "influencers" off the back of global social media audiences. For introverts, this personal brand world can be highly challenging. But it is getting harder to avoid. Here are a few thoughts on keeping brand "you" healthy and authentic.

What is your personal brand?

Your personal brand is effectively what people think when your name is mentioned. It includes the following –

- The way you exert influence without even being there
- The way you use your expertise and opportunities to influence others
- The way you dress and present yourself
- The value you are perceived to bring to the world

Why is it important?

Jobs and careers are radically changing. Many people have a collection of pursuits rather than a job and have a broader personal and professional positioning beyond their vocations. The digital revolution has made individuals more visible (and searchable). In many contexts, without a digital profile, we barely exist. If you recognise the inevitable reality of having a personal brand, it makes sense to embrace it and use it to your advantage. Things you can do include:

Know your Google self

You can pretty much guarantee that before anybody meets you or interviews you, they will Google you. The way you show up in a Google search is an important first impression. You should Google yourself regularly, so you are aware of what your Google self looks like.

If you are not happy with what you see, upgrade your proactive digital activity. Your LinkedIn profile is a good place to start. And it is relatively inexpensive to start your own website if you have enough content for that.

Have a good pitch

Most days somebody will ask you what you do. The answer should always be ready. Don't just say what job you do. Think about what drives and motivates you, what you "really" do in your professional and networked life and other things about you and your experiences that make you intriguing. Once you have this, you also have your introductory paragraph for LinkedIn and your biography for next time somebody needs one.

Think about your point-of-difference skills

There is a great body of research by Professor Ruth Bridgstock and others that looks at our evolution from T-shaped skills to key-shaped skills. In other words, instead of just having a wide range of general skills and one very deep expertise, we now tend to need three or four high level skills to be able to adapt well in the contemporary workforce. You need to know what yours are. If you do not have them, you need to get them and ensure your profiles and resumes reflect them well.

Communicate your value

I have read hundreds of CVs and job application letters over the years and the vast bulk of them are a history lesson in what people have done. What I really want to know is what value candidates bring. That is a very different thing.

Like any branding, your personal brand comes down to your compelling points of difference as an individual. You will have plenty when you properly self-analyze. Think deeply about what value you bring to a workplace, and the world, and talk about that with passion. Do this, and your real personal brand will come through.

Stand for something

Your personal brand includes the things you are passionate about. If you feel strongly about something important, people should associate that with you. If you articulate the things you care about enough, you will manage to be influential even when you are not in the room. Once your brand exists without your physical presence, you will know you have left a real mark in the cosmos. You might find the guide below useful in discovering and setting your personal brand.

YOUR PERSONAL BRAND PROFILE

Your pitch
The three things you say about yourself when you meet people, your compelling "selling" propositions and the value you bring to the world

Your blurb
Two to three sentences that would best describe your personal brand and your personal story

Your key skills
The three to four things that you are best at or known for

What you stand for
The things you are most passionate about

Your style
The way you dress and the way you seek to present yourself to the world

Your networks
The main groups or "tribes" you associate with

Your links
Links to your social media and broader digital profiles

Your personal brand framework
Your attributes, the benefits you bring to others, your values, and your personality traits

Your brand essence
Two to three words that sum up the heart of who you are

9. The myths of career progression

If you look at a trend line on the performance of the Australian stock exchange since the 1950s, it shows a beautiful, steady ascension and a lot of people getting progressively wealthier as they sit on the veranda sipping Nespresso coffee and eating tofu.

However, if you put the full data that drives the trend line onto the same grid, you see a very different story. Underneath the steady line are wild fluctuations, occasional full-throttle crashes and a recipe for nervousness for those relying heavily on shares for their livelihoods.

Careers are a bit the same. When we are young, and particularly if we are ambitious, we tend to imagine a nice steady career line across our lives. It culminates in a very senior role and finishes with a gold watch and a nice speech as you are ushered off into retirement.

As you get older, you begin to realise that careers are seldom a measured climb up an undulating slope. They are more like a game of Super Mario Brothers – dodging pitfalls, moments of rapid acceleration followed by obstacles you can't get past, wild creatures jumping out at you from unexpected places, and occasionally running out of lives and having to start again.

There is nothing wrong with this. It is part of the adventure of life. It only becomes a problem if we see the Super Mario experience as a fail or proof that we have not lived up to expectations.

So, from the "if I knew then what I know now" file, I offer the following myths on career progression.

Myth 1 - Careers just keep advancing with time and experience

If the career progression line we imagined in our youth was accurate, our most senior roles would not come along until well into our 50s and we would be in our most senior roles when we retire. The reality is typically far different.

Most research suggests the peak salary years for people is between the ages of 48 and 54. In a fast-changing world, many people are reaching the most senior roles much earlier than that and the leadership landscape tends to be dominated by people in their 40s. In the technology world there are plenty of CEOs aged in their 30s and even 20s. All of this group have many decades still to work and there aren't too many rungs left on the advancement ladder. They have a choice of a long flat line in a senior role, or eventually finding a totally different approach to careers, or prioritising bigger picture issues outside of the corporate world.

There is also an issue of mathematics. The number of people who aspire to be CEOs and the number of CEO jobs available don't add up. The stark reality is that not everybody who wants to get to the top can get there and career progression can be an accident of history and luck – being in the right place at the right time with the right skills and the right cheer squad.

I personally came to the conclusion in my early 50s that I had actually achieved everything I set out to do in my career and still had at least 20 years of work ahead of me. I made the decision then to chase challenges and jobs that ticked the boxes on what I enjoyed doing rather than trying to work out where I was in a hierarchy. It is quite an empowering thing to do.

Myth 2 - You should go into management to advance your career

One of the saddest things you see in corporations is a miserable manager. These are typically people who loved their vocation, accepted a promotion into a management role because they wanted the money and status and then endured a working life of total misery.

One of the hardest truths for any ambitious person to face is that they are not cut out for management – they either dislike or get stressed by managing others or they just don't have the emotional intelligence to deal with people. These people need to realise that being in senior management and success do not necessarily go hand in hand. The world is full of very successful lone wolfs or people who work for themselves rather than face the challenges of juggling the myriad of human foibles inherent in management.

Equally sad is watching people who get promoted a level past their competence point, or optimal work happiness point, and struggle along unhappily because the annoying career voice in their head tells them that advancing up the ladder is the right thing to do.

Many are also under pressure at home to keep dialling up the dollars. I think being honest about our optimal satisfaction level in the work chain is one of the most important things we can do for ourselves. Little good ever came from misery.

Myth 3 - Changing jobs equates with rapid advancement

This is actually seldom true. Job changes that allow people to use their experience to take a logical next step in their career (and when they are blocked in a lane at their current organisation) have positive results. So do job changes that give you a lot of stretch and growth room rather than just replicating what you are already doing.

Beyond that, there is little evidence. In fact, Jim Collins' *Good to Great* research suggested the most successful company leaders were generally internal appointments with a very good knowledge of the business and its history. Another study I read a few years ago (can't remember the source) found that one of the key attributes of the most successful companies was having a management team who had worked together for many years and were very robust and adept at making decisions together – quickly and effectively.

There is nothing wrong with changing jobs. I've certainly done it lots of times. The danger is in changing jobs for the sake of it or based on a mistaken belief that it is the only path to success.

Myth 4 - There is a logic to what people get paid

You would generally expect in a marketplace that similar jobs get similar pay. In senior ranks in many companies it is not that simple. For example, very talented individuals with unique or special skills very often get paid more than the people who are managing them.

I have personally been in roles where my deputy has been paid more than me. Companies rely on supply-demand discussions with non-award staff being secretive, so the value placed on an individual does not have to follow a hierarchy of logic. In 2013 there was a huge furore within the ranks of Australia's national broadcaster (the Australian Broadcasting Corporation) when the salaries of senior staff and presenters was leaked to the media. You could pretty much guarantee the same thing would happen in every organisation if salaries were public knowledge.

Even between organisations there are vast differences. International firms will quite often pay more because they have equity in salaries across geographies. Others pay more simply because they increased the scale at some stage of their evolution to attract better people and that just locked in. There is little logic to it. It is basic supply and demand, accidents of history and ad-hoc negotiations around attracting or keeping individuals.

I have personally accepted salary drops of up to 30% doing jobs of similar status. Ultimately you have to decide if you are chasing the challenge or chasing the money.

Myth 5 - You need to work for someone else

I sincerely hope this has changed now, but when I went through the education system, every career conversation was about working for somebody else. I never once heard anyone discuss the genuine career option of starting a business. When I look back at my cohorts, the only ones who went into business in their 20s and 30s came from families with a history of running businesses.

In Australia, a country dominated by small (even micro) businesses, learning the secrets of business and entrepreneurialism should be a key plank of the education system. Thankfully immigrants have brought a strong enterprise culture to this country but we are still miles behind other parts of the world in creating an ecosystem that encourages young people to back their ideas based on a solid understanding of strategy, markets and business principles.

Thankfully a lot of people opt to start businesses later in life or as a retirement wind-down strategy. Better late than never. There is still a dead zone in the peak working years when people want to start businesses, but the risks are too great against the drain of mortgages and school fees.

Financial adviser Paul Clitheroe was instrumental in broadening the mindset on working and finances in

Australia through a 1990s television program called *Money*. In one of his early books Clitheroe said the secret of his business's initial success was an agreement that none of the directors would draw a salary for some time so the cash flow got a chance to grow before the costs mounted (they relied on working partners to pay the bills). This is not possible for everyone, but people running their own businesses on their own terms often seem to enjoy their success more than those just creating success for a faceless entity.

Be true to yourself about your career aspirations

I suspect ultimately the career hierarchy measures we tend to default to are the wrong ones to judge a working life. If we all measured success purely on a job satisfaction index, the rest would probably fall into place. Professor Chris Leaver from Oxford University told the G20 Brisbane Global Cafe event in 2014 that if you had enough food to eat you had many problems but if you had no food you only had one problem. The more complex our lives, the more demanding we are of ourselves and the more we create a financial beast that needs to be fed, the more we create pressure to climb the ladder.

Sometimes it is better to get off the ladder and just turn around and admire the view. If you sit a while, you might just get used to it.

10. Avoiding the biggest career mistakes

I was once asked to list the biggest mistakes I had made in my career.

It was not something I had thought about before. I tend to try to stay positive and concentrate on future opportunities rather than past failures.

The following are my personal observations on the biggest career mistakes people make. And, yes, at various times I have made all of them.

Taking the wrong job because you feel flattered

There are two types of jobs – the ones you find and the ones that find you. The ones you find are a conscious choice and they are generally based on some version of a career plan.

The ones that find you are out of the blue and they come with a powerful sense of flattery. Somebody has singled you out to offer you a job – you. It is such a good feeling that many people accept jobs just because of that. Only to realise all too soon that it is a bad move.

It is nice to be wanted. But if the job is inconsistent with your life and career plan it can end badly.

Not doing enough diligence

Employment engagement surveys consistently show that

the mismatch between the promise of a job when you take it and the reality of it is a major source of disgruntlement and disengagement.

It is easy to blame the company. But companies "sell" like everybody else. When they are trying to attract the best candidates, they are putting their spin on the role.

While companies have an obligation to be honest and upfront about roles they are offering, it is also up to us to check roles out properly ourselves. It isn't hard to track down people (usually someone you know) who can give you a frank warts-and-all assessment of what you are getting yourself into. I am always amazed at how few people do this. And they pay for it later.

If it sounds too good to be true, it probably is

Sometimes we get job offers that are just so good on paper, we feel we need to take them. It might pay an incredible amount, come with lots of perks or promise extra holidays and flexibility.

If you are lucky, it will all work out as imagined. However, in many cases, the old adage that if it sounds too good to be true, it probably is, will probably prove correct.

I have been caught out badly on this, even when I thought I had done diligence. At the very least, if you are faced with a "too good to be true' scenario you should take the opportunity with a healthy degree of scepticism. If you are pleasantly surprised, that's great. If not, at least you will have factored in the possibility of being duped.

Confusing a bad patch with a fundamental problem

Most jobs go through seasons. In good economies with interesting projects on the go and great managers in the top jobs, your employment can feel like it is covered with fairy dust and you feel energised and happy.

But the stars don't always align, and you can wake up one day and find your once great job has turned foul. Often this doesn't mean it is fundamentally broken. It could be just one new contract or one senior appointment away from getting back on track. It is often worth being a bit patient through the down cycles and looking for your positive energy outside of work. I've seen plenty of people leave great jobs for this reason and regret it later. And eggs are really hard to unscramble once you have cooked them.

Underestimating your ability to make a job better

It seems most employees blame managers and this mythical creature known as "the company" or "they" if they perceive their job to be going badly. The reality of most jobs is that you know more about what you do than anybody else, managers included. You are the only one waking up every morning thinking specifically about your particular job.

There is a good chance that you know exactly what is needed to make it right and that you have a lot more power than you realise to do something about it. Most managers get presented with problems but would much rather be presented with solutions from people with the right knowledge. That is mostly you. It is always a good idea to try to solve your own problems before you try to delegate them up.

Letting a job rule your life

No matter how much you love your job, if you let it totally rule your life you can almost guarantee you will eventually start to resent it. You may sign up to 12-hour days or some sort of super-commute with your eyes fully open but one day you will inevitably ask "why am I doing this?" and you won't remember the answer.

If you find a great job that you want to do for a long time, by definition it needs to be sustainable. There is little point working yourself to death even in a job that you love. Loving a job is all the more reason to insist that you can do it in tune with your life balance. Just because you enjoy your work doesn't mean you don't want to do anything else in your life.

If you have time to do the things you like to do outside of work and you enjoy your work, you are better off than more than 70% of other people. And you won't let the job rule your life. You will stay in charge and set positive habits from the start.

Having the same year every year

We all tend to be creatures of habit. That makes us susceptible to repeating what we have done before and slipping into templates that prevent us having to come up with new approaches. It is easy to get caught in cycles that feel like that. If you are doing the same things at the same time every year eventually you will probably start to feel like you are just going through the motions. The banality of that can really get you down.

I'm a big fan of having a plan at the start of each year. Even people who are not ambitious usually need some sense of growth and positive momentum each year. You have to go looking for this. You need to take charge of your own life and career. Nobody else is going to do that for you.

11. Facing fear and taking risks

"He'd learned long ago that a life lived without risks pretty much wasn't worth living. Life rewarded courage, even when that first step was taken neck-deep in fear."
 - **Tamera Alexander** (from *Within My Heart*)

For humans, fear can be our biggest strength and our biggest weakness. Our brains are wired to fear things, for good reason. Without fear we would do stupid things, take crazy risks and probably die young.

There is, however, a downside to this. We have little control of where our fear meter is set. The same brain function that keeps us safe can also stop us taking positive risks. If we listen too much to the little voice of fear in our heads, we can end up doing very little. Certainly in the workplace it can mean keeping our head down and avoiding getting into trouble or putting forward ideas. This can also mean never pushing ourselves, never living up to our potential and never feeling the adrenalin rush of a slightly risky venture that we manage to pull off.

In books like this, we are often told to take risks. Quote books are full of advice on taking the plunge. Helen Keller said, "Life is either a daring adventure or nothing at all". Ralph Waldo Emerson said, "Don't be too timid and squeamish about your actions. All life is an experiment. The more experiments you make the better".

Perhaps the most powerful quote of all comes from the Bard himself (William Shakespeare): "A coward dies a thousand times before his death, but the valiant taste of death but once. It seems to me most strange that men should fear, seeing that death, a necessary end, will come when it will come." Basically, Shakespeare was saying that if you feared things all the time, you had to live with that stress and angst over and over. If you are realistic about risks and they are calculated, you need to only suffer when things go wrong.

In general, unless you are reckless, you will make more good decisions than bad. If you are pushing ideas within your skills and experience, they are probably on solid ground and following a well-honed gut instinct in the deep areas of your brain.

In the game of risk, there are a few key questions you should ask:

- What is the worst that could happen?
- If the worst thing happens, will I be able to survive that?

- Will I feel better if I do this and fail or I don't even try?

If you take a risk and things go south, you can ask:

- Did anybody die or get seriously injured?
- Did I learn from the experience?
- Will the things I have learnt help me make better decisions in the future?

In many work environments, I have been astounded at how strong the anti-risk cultures can be and how powerful the naysayer voices are in nuking ideas. People are quick to identify what can go wrong as a reason not to try in the first place. Yet, if we lived our life trying to set the risk dial at zero, we would do very little. We might as well be dead. You would pretty much have to stay in bed all day. But, even then, Deep Vein Thrombosis would probably kill you.

In contrast to this anti-risk culture in many companies, there are other environments where failure is very much part of the process. In science, there can be years of trial and error before breakthroughs happen. In these environments, you inevitably have to fail along the way to ultimately succeed.

Sportspeople take risks all the time. Roger Federer could not have become one of the greatest players of all time without taking some risks with big shots or serves at crucial points. No race driver can take the chequered flag without taking some risks and passing other drivers.

Many of our most successful entrepreneurs took enormous risks to achieve their accomplishments. Sometimes it could have gone either way. But they backed themselves based on instincts and experience.

There is no right or wrong with risk taking and everyone needs to be true to their own fear voice. Some people love to fly while some are terrified. Some people can't wait to bungy jump. Others would never dream of doing it. Some people give up their jobs to try their luck as an artist. Others need the safe harbour of a solid, regular income.

There is no universal right and wrong in this area. Given that, the only real way to grapple with the dilemma is through a risk mitigation plan. It is far more empowering to take a risk if you have considered carefully all the things that might go wrong and you have a plan to either reduce the likelihood of that or minimise that damage when it happens.

With this approach, not only do you take surprise out the equation, you genuinely empower yourself to try some stuff in the comfort that you have a Plan B if needed.

Of course, the danger in so many gurus telling us to take more risks is that we end up with too many people doing that and too much collateral damage. Stupid risks are still just that.

I often see people in the start-up space with really great ideas who put their life savings and their house on the line and lose everything. They learn the hard way that great ideas are not a guarantee of success. You also need a large enough market of people who are actually prepared to pay for your great idea, and you need enough cash flow to sustain early losses. Some of the best ideas fail miserably. Start-ups are exciting but the stats suggest they are not for the faint-hearted.

In a corporate setting it is always worth asking yourself if you would invest in something if it was your own money. If the answer if a genuine yes, you can push your idea with confidence.

In this context, another hard truth we need to face is that not all of our ideas are good or even the best in our workplaces. We all need to have the courage to kill off a bad idea, particularly if the bad idea is our own. It is one thing to have a good idea and fail. That is life and business. Failing in the blind pursuit of a bad idea is far less defensible.

12. Making decisions in a half right world

"Trying to please everybody is impossible – if you did that, you'd end up in the middle with nobody liking you. You've just got to make the decision about what you think is your best and do it."
  - **John Lennon** (Musician and song writer)

Right and wrong used to seem like such simple concepts. You hear both sides, you weigh up the arguments and you decide who is right.

Easy right? Well, not really. The older I get the more I realise that this is a really naïve view. On many issues there is no definitive right or wrong, or universal truth.

We mostly live in a world where, on many core issues, everybody is half-right (or at least part-right). Once you recognise that, it throws the nature of decision-making into something of a funk. And often we have a choice of picking a decision that might, at best, keep 50% of people happy. Or we can compromise and do something that makes everybody a bit happy but produces a largely meaningless result.

Increasingly over the years I have found myself in corporate settings arguing 60-40 decisions – "We did this because there is a 60% upside and a 40% downside". Faced with a choice, you always go with the 60%. But 40% is still a heck of downside.

I fear that public debate is too often practiced at extremes. One group argues black, the other argues white. One argues left, the other argues right. One argues up, one argues down.

All of their views are well considered and argued. And mostly those listening to the debate are really none the wiser because both sides cannot possibly be right.

This is particularly stark in the environmental debate where public discourse seems to happen mostly at the extreme points – the planet is dying at one end and climate change is a fraud at the other. Inevitably the truth is stuck somewhere in the middle looking for a friend.

One of the most thought-provoking pieces of commentary I have heard on climate change came some years ago from the then Origin Energy Managing Director Grant King. He argued that meeting carbon emission targets was effectively a "practical problem for practical people" rather than an issue for zealots at both extremes.

This is a good way of looking at many of the complex issues we face. The fate of the planet will ultimately be in the hands of engineers, scientists and decision-makers who can seek solutions based on impartial evidence, sensible behaviour change and technological innovation.

Similarly, international harmony and global peace will rely on decent, well-meaning people understanding the world from another vantage point and trying to see solutions based on mutual interest rather than self-interest.

Solving world hunger and poverty will come down to enough people believing that a greater humanity is more important than one based on live and let die.

Perhaps we need to stop asking who is right or wrong and ask questions like these instead:

1. What outcome will produce the best outcome for the most people?
2. What is the actual problem we are trying to solve? Let's make sure we are really working on that.
3. What happens if we do nothing?

4. Who is really best qualified to make the judgement?
5. Will the benefits really outweigh the collateral damage?

We also need to seek out the views of genuinely objective people who can look at practical problems with fresh eyes and come up with the best solutions based on the highest quality information.

Simple right? Well, not really. It might just be half right.

13. Fixing problems by changing your vantage point

There is a movie called *Vantage Point* in which the same story is played over and over and each time you see it from a different person's perspective. And each time the same story looks totally different.

The world in general is like that. Every view and situation looks different depending on where you are sitting and the disposition you bring to that view. This was depicted brilliantly in the classic 1957 jury room drama *12 Angry Men*.

Workplaces are no different. Most offices are full of "issues" and little frictions that have to be sorted. Sometimes these issues get heated and personal and create long-term fractures in the workforce or between individuals. In some cases, they are the origins of factions and deep-seated office politics.

When this happens, issues soon start getting assessed on politics rather than merit and toxins spread through the office and make everyone's life complicated (i.e. miserable). One of the hardest things for any person to do is to genuinely consider what an issue looks like from somebody else's perspective. But it is amazing how different things can look when you really make an effort to understand the world from another person's vantage point.

Here are some thoughts on this.

Consider you could be wrong

Could this be possible? Um, yes. A lot. We all get caught up having a view and arguing it. After a while we start prosecuting a case rather than looking at things objectively. I try hard to consider that the annoying person who is disagreeing with me just may be right. And it has saved me making a lot of big mistakes.

Consider that you might both be half right

As outlined in the previous chapter, the biggest problem in any issue, work or otherwise, is what I call "Half Right Syndrome". Few issues are black and white or right and wrong. They are mostly somewhere in the middle. It is often dangerous to look for a clean solution to everything. Issues that have many shades of grey may need more complex solutions that recognise that neither side is right or wrong. They are both half right.

Consider that you are actors in a play

It is easy to confuse healthy, robust internal debate with a perception that particular people are at war with each other. In most workplaces we have an individual role to play and that involves advocating internally based on the part we have in the corporate performance. That does not mean two areas are at war. It means both are robustly arguing a case, so all relevant points are considered. If there is a sound management process, someone further up the line will be able to assess both sides of a healthy debate and make the call based on what is best for the company. That is a characteristic of a system that is working, not broken.

Consider the other person's motivation

Part of seeing an issue from somebody else's vantage point, is understanding their motivation for having a particular view. Some people just feel strongly about something or have a "difficult" personality. But mostly there is an underlying motivation – they are worried about their job and future, they are worried about their budget, they have put their heart and soul into something, and they do not want to give it up, they had a bad experience in the past with the idea you are suggesting etc. etc. Police always look for motive first when they investigate a crime. It helps to do the same when you are caught up in a disagreement.

SECTION 3

Recapturing your life balance

"We need to do a better job of putting ourselves higher on our own to-do list."
- **Michelle Obama** (United States attorney, author and former First Lady)

I meet very few people who believe their life is truly balanced. Most describe some version of a battle for equilibrium. Every so often you feel like the scales of life are balanced, but the balance is precarious and barely a breath of wind away from returning to topsy turvy.

This section provides some thoughts on achieving a sense of balance and contentment, or at least accepting the transitory nature of relentless ocean waves and learning to ride them rather than fight them.

1. The work and life divide

For decades we have talked about work-life balance and the difficulties achieving that in a complex world.

The old notions of a rigid 9-5 day have broken down in most professional work settings. So have set lunch hours and morning tea breaks, and the notion of clocking in and clocking out.

In professional roles, paid overtime is mostly something from the past and most of us in senior positions are paid to deliver an outcome rather than paid to do a certain number of hours that are counted and supervised.

Add to that the proliferation of the smart "super phone" and always-on technology and the thin black line between our work and home lives becomes so blurred we can barely see it.

There are a few ways of looking at this.

We can consider it a problem and put a whole lot of habits in place to redraw the line. Or we can roll with it and stop getting stressed about things we cannot control. I think it is time to stop talking about work-life balance and start to just talk about "life balance".

If you really hate your job, you should look for another one. If you quite like your job, you might as well embrace that and try to get as much satisfaction as you can from it.

Life balance is about using the precious time we have well. Projecting forward, it also means living a life of our choosing and hoping we can look back in the future with no regrets.

When viewed through this lens, work does not need to be

totally in the chore section. Instead we should all be seeking jobs that we enjoy and that enhance our life experiences.

As a kid I was told that a balanced life consisted of eight hours work, eight hours sleep, and eight hours play in every 24 hours.

These fundamentals are still sound in many respects. Eight hours sleep is healthy and paid work is still mostly structured around eight-hour days. The challenge is the "play". With working households increasingly categorised by two people in the paid workforce, the fundamentals have changed. In a different era, a man might go to work for eight hours while his spouse/partner did similar hours working on "home duties". In theory, this left quite a few hours for both to socialise, watch the evening television, pursue hobbies and take part in community activities.

The labour force participation has risen sharply over the past 40 years but home maintenance, household administration and childcare still need to be done outside of the eight hours of "work". This has been coupled with working hours creep for most professionals in white collar occupations as well as long commutes and constant connectivity through technology.

The end-result is very little rest or play between work and sleep. The old saying says that "all work and no play makes Jack a dull boy". There is a real danger that in contemporary society we are all becoming dull boys and girls, emotionally and physically drained by the grind.

What's more, most of the social research suggests that humans have less friends than in the past and, aside from the pseudo friendships and connections we make on social media, our face-to-face social interactions and community engagements are in decline.

There is plenty of research connecting strong social and community engagement with positive mental and physical health. Put all this together and there is something wrong with the picture. If you accept that the life balance for most working people is out of whack, then clearly we need to find the reset button. This will not happen centrally or through government action. Ultimately people will need to restore their own balance. The time has come to think. To really think. To ask ourselves some tough questions and take some time to reboot and plan for a better future.

It is time to ask things like:

- Are you doing what makes you happy? What can you do now to pursue your passion? How can you emerge stronger and more satisfied with life?
- What are you grateful for? It might be time to really think about that.
- What have you stopped doing that previously gave you great joy?

2. It only takes one thing

Wisdom often comes from the most unexpected of sources. I have long been intrigued by the philosophy of a character called Curly in the 1991 comedy *City Slickers*. In the film, Billy Crystal plays a radio advertising salesman facing disillusionment with life and his job "selling air". He embarks on a cattle drive to find his smile and bring some perspective back into his life.

In an unexpected scene, Crystal sought the wisdom of the hard-nosed and intimidating cattle drive leader Curly (played by Jack Palance) on how to deal with the sink holes that had formed in his life. Curly provided the simplest answer on the secret of happiness: "One thing."

Crystal is naturally confused by the answer and Curly, who dies a bit later in the movie, does not elaborate. Eventually Crystal realises what Curly meant. Everyone just needs one thing to put meaning and genuine happiness into their lives. The trick is to find it.

But the one thing can be different for each of us. If you look at people around you, it seems that the happiest of them are the ones who have found the "one thing" that makes them happy – our "element" as Ken Robinson beautifully articulated in his book of the same name.

Proactively chasing your element

If you let it happen, life's default position is spending most of your time doing things you don't want to do. This is not a great use of your life. As a rough calculation I would say only about 30% of people I know are doing something they are really passionate about. The rest have settled and are doing what they have to do to get by.

Sadly, the pressures of living costs, responsibilities and the infrastructure we build around "normal" lives locks most people into a daily grind that is hard to escape.

Albert Einstein is widely quoted as saying that if you turn your passion into a job, you never have to work a day in your life. This should be everyone's objective.

The question, of course, is how. I think the starting point is not assuming your main pursuit and your job are necessarily the same thing.

I spent many years working in the media, and it has always been notoriously hard to get your first break into journalism. At the first large newspaper I worked for, we took on about five cadets every year from literally hundreds of applicants. Over the years I have been asked many times how to "break in" to journalism. My answer was always the same. You are already empowered to be a journalist. You just need to activate that power.

What I meant was, if people really wanted to write as their passion, they could do it. They could write stories and cover things. That is not the same as having a job in journalism. You still need money to live. However, there is nothing stopping you (particularly when you are young) from working at your passion during the day or at night and using the other zone of the day to work a job to pay your bills.

Pretty much everyone I know who has taken that approach to their passion, and who has genuine talent, has ended up also making money from their passion.

If you believe you were put on Earth for a reason, it seems like it should be almost an obligation to contribute that passion back to the world. Otherwise, as a human race, we are underselling our potential. Not to mention having a population who are half as happy as they might be.

3. The death of the twilight zone

Do you ever get a feeling that something is missing? You know, the sensation you get when your wallet isn't in your pocket, you are not entirely sure where you put your keys, or you have a nagging sense that you were supposed to be somewhere else.

I fear that for a lot of us many of our days have become like that. And it is because so many of us have lost our "twilight zone," that magical period between the end of work and the start of the evening eat/prepare-for-tomorrow/sleep zone once known as weekday discretionary time.

If you examine Australian time-use statistics, it is evident that, from 1992 and 2006, there was a fundamental shift in the nature of our daily "transition" time.

One thing in particular stood out – time spent on weekday socialisation and community activities fell by about two-thirds. In other words, our twilight zone was shrinking like the ozone layer.

The anecdotal evidence is everywhere:

- Service clubs struggling to find members, leaders and volunteers who are not retired from work
- Busy mothers and fathers trying desperately to finish work assignments, pick up children, make meals and then get something resembling proper sleep
- In many countries more than 20% of full-time employees working more than 50-hour weeks
- Peak-hour traffic conditions that stretch across 2-3 hours
- Evening airports full of businesspeople day-tripping between states
- Growth in after-work functions and professional networking events among the growing professional and managerial classes
- Constantly wired employees whose work and home lives blur into a perpetual bing of emails, texts and meeting requests.

And on it goes…

The decline of the traditional weekday recreational fringe zone could easily be written off as an inevitable consequence of a globalised economy and tighter economic conditions.

But curiously the change largely happened during one of the best runs of economic circumstances in a century.

I suspect the real culprit is options. We are all trying to cram in too much and discretionary time in our "twilight zone" has become a casualty. Perhaps even more concerning is that it appears social, community and family time may have been the biggest losers.

I am often reminded of the Malcolm Gladwell book *Outliers* and the medical miracle that was Roseto, Pennsylvania. The town of 1500 people had exceptionally low rates of major chronic health disorders. Doctors looked for the secret in geography and diet but found it in community. The best answer seemed to be that being part of an extraordinarily close-knit and highly socialised community was very beneficial for our well-being.

Yet this seems to be the very thing we are opting to throw out of the balloon basket when the options weigh us down.

I remember a fascinating research finding from AustraliaSCAN social analyst David Chalke showing that, around 2005, Australians started to regard choice as a negative. Too much choice was becoming stressful.

Just 20 years earlier, high school economics classes were telling us that having a lot of choice was an indicator of high living standards. How times change.

Perhaps, in the future, all activities might have to come with a health warning that says too much choice is bad for you. And bringing back the twilight zone from extinction might be the remedy.

4. Time – our most precious gift

I suspect very few people look back on their lives and think they made the best use of the time they had. It is also likely that, if we were given the date of our death in advance, all of us would probably do a lot of things differently.

Charles Darwin was a stickler for using each day well and getting the right mix between work and leisure. He said: "A man who dares to waste one hour of time has not discovered the value of life".

There seems to be a general consensus that time is moving more quickly than in the past and we never have enough of it to provide us with a sense that we are in control and will get everything done.

Of course, time is still moving at the same speed. The problem is humans. Not all that many decades ago, humans seemed to have a simpler set of options. As a child growing up in a country town in the 1960s and 1970s, days seemed to go on forever. That is also the last time I remember ever waking up and thinking – there is absolutely nothing I have to do today. Sometimes I really wish I could have that feeling again.

The problem we have is options creep. There are now so many things we can do in our day. The Internet connects us with literally everything in the world. We have all the options of the past, plus several million more. However, the one dynamic we can never change is the number of hours there are in a day. So we just try to cram more and more into those precious hours.

In the end the only choice we have is to treat prioritisation as our most important skill. We will never have any more hours in our day. The question that matters is how we should best use them.

5. Breaking out of a rut

Every day I take an early morning walk or run. And I pass pretty much the same people at the same place at the same time each day. Sometimes this genuinely freaks me out.

It would not surprise me if I started waking up each morning to *I Got You Babe* by Sonny and Cher and Bill Murray jumped from behind a tree to tell me about Punxsutawney Phil's weather predictions for the season. (See *Groundhog Day* and changing the route on page 112).

It is so easy to get stuck in a rut. Most of us are creatures of routine and find comfort and security from that. The danger with ruts is that you can end up living the same day every day rather than living fresh days with new experiences and people.

That can leave us feeling like life has become passé and we are going through the motions rather than constantly building something new and exciting.

Feeling trapped by routine? Here are some thoughts on how to break out of it.

Plan a break from whatever you do

I was talking to someone in the entertainment industry some time ago and he pointed out that his industry was all about people needing a break from whatever they did, even a break from doing very little.

If you are retired, you need a break from that, or you get stale and frozen by inertia. Even if you are doing something everyday that you love, you still need a break from it occasionally to really appreciate how much you enjoy it.

For most of us, daily routine is about work and holding a household together. The statistics show huge numbers of people don't take their holidays. This is not healthy. It is not only important to have regular recharge and refresh breaks; it is also vital that we plan them. Always having something to look forward to is a big part of rut breaking.

Create some novel experiences

The importance of novel experiences came starkly into the spotlight during the COVID-19 pandemic. Lockdowns and restrictions scaled back options on what we could do in our days. In many cases it took a working day with a variety of activities and interactions and replaced it with hours staring at video screens.

In the absence of automatic novel experiences, we have to be a lot more proactive in planning them.

This can mean plotting mid-week social experiences with

family or friends. I meet a lot of people who say that their Monday to Friday is programmed, and they totally rely on the weekend for novel experiences. Putting some spice into the mid-week can help add lustre to the routine.

My favourite weeks are the ones when I do a movie or a concert mid-week (something of a carryover from being a kid and the apparent decadence of staying up late on a 'school night').

Create a new habit

Conventional wisdom suggests that it takes three weeks to form a habit and about three months to lock it in. This requires you to start at some point.

If you are stuck in ruts and routines that are getting you down, you need to change the habit now. Not next week. Not next month. Not next year.

You also need to schedule the new habit in your day, the same way you schedule meetings and meals. As *The 7 Habits of Highly Effective People* author Stephen R. Covey says, it is about scheduling priorities (including new ones) not just scheduling the usual routine. Then you have to accept that you might have to fight the strong forces of rutdom for months before your change of habit is locked in. That is okay. You can do that.

Change the vantage point

The world can look completely different, depending on where you are sitting. Changing your vantage point can help you see the same world and the same life in a completely different light.

This can mean trying a different coffee shop, proactively catching up with some different people, taking a different approach to your job if you are getting bored, and just mixing things up a bit.

Change the route

If you walk or run, there is something comforting about taking the same route every day. There is also something unnerving about it.

Groundhog Day is typically referenced as a movie about a man who is stuck in the same day every day.

The reality of the movie is that, even though he is stuck in the same day, Bill Murray's character lives that same day differently every time. He cannot control how others live their days, but he can change his own.

What's more, the longer he lives the same day but changes what he does in the day, the better his life becomes. The real lesson from *Groundhog Day* is our ability to control our own script even in a world that is scripted around us.

And the more we mix up the routine, the deeper becomes our life experience. When we are old, it will be interesting to look back and ask if we have lived tens of thousands of days, or we have lived the same day tens of thousands of times.

6. The life advice I wish I had at 25

I have generally found that life is a series of contradictions. Most of us are wired to aspire to things that we deep down know don't really make us happy. As we get older, we start to realise that much of our career positioning and aspirations are based on an artificial construct of success. So many people never pursue things they really want to do because they are locked in a maze and can't find the exit.

Sometimes this is due to fear. Sometimes we live our lives based on the expectations of others.

I keep a list of life lessons so I can refer back to them regularly on days when I need a boost or a gentle reminder about the things that really matter. These are some life lessons for my 25-year-old self.

Stop worrying about what others think

You will spend a lot of time worrying what other people think. After a while you realise that if you are true to your values and happy with who you are, it really doesn't matter what other people think of you. In fact, as Deepak Chopra observed, it is probably none of your business.

This is a sub-set of the all-too-regular refusal of people to be true to themselves. Instead of doing things they know in their heart of hearts to be right, they construct their lives based on what others might think. This is bizarre and very, very common.

One of the greatest freedoms anyone can experience is the freedom to rid themselves of concern about how they are regarded. We are obsessed with ourselves because we are what we've got. Other people aren't nearly as concerned with us as we often think and frankly most of them have not earned the right to make judgments about us. Oscar Wilde reminded us that we have to be ourselves – everybody else is taken. If we are happy with who we are, why do we give so much weight to the opinion of others? It makes little sense.

Fixing the things you can fix

There are various versions of this based on ancient Buddhist philosophy. Many people say their lives were transformed when they finally learned to quickly fix the worrying things they could control and stop worrying over the things they could not control. The one thing we can control is how we react to every situation.

If you are worried about something, fix it quickly if you control it, and stop being dragged down by things you can't change.

Choosing optimism

We often default to finding the negative in things. But even Winston Churchill, who battled chronic lows throughout his life, famously said he chose to be an optimist because none of the other options made much sense. He was right. Choosing to be negative really doesn't make any sense.

Ultimately, we always have a choice to go glass half empty or half full. It seems that the people who are happiest, and who live longest, decide to take the optimistic path. Most clouds have silver linings. Or at least the clouds eventually pass.

Being flexible

There is a great line in the Jewel Kilcher song *Innocence Maintained* that says: "Nature has a funny way of breaking what does not bend". How true. In fact, if you think about it, the most difficult issues we tend to face are the ones where everyone is dug in on a point and not prepared to budge. In these circumstances, things do tend to break. If you look at nature, everything is about flexibility and adapting to environments as they change. We are all part of nature, so it makes sense that adaptability should also be part of how we live and work.

A lawyer told me once that he hated mediation because it suggested everything could be compromised. He preferred the idea of a single argument or case being ruled as superior. However, by definition, this means if we cannot reach a compromise, we lose any control of the outcome. As outlined in Section Two, in reality we mostly live in a world where everyone is half right on most issues. If we are prepared to be flexible and listen to all views, often we find our position was not the best one anyway.

Taking risks early

Up until very recently, the average age of a start-up

entrepreneur in Australia was about 35. In Silicon Valley it is about 25. The trouble with starting things at 35 is that most people already have a lot of life overheads, family responsibilities and debt.

It is good to take some calculated risks at any age (within reason) but young people are often best placed to do this. They can try things with lower risk and overheads and can fail early and often without smashing their lives apart.

As the span of life extends, youth takes on an even more exciting dimension. For emerging generations likely to work into their eighties, the early years have a lot more scope for career and business experimentation. This should be encouraged. Society can only change for the better when innovative people have the time and freedom to try new things.

Accepting your own version of normal

The word normal is overused. There is no such thing as a normal anything. Everyone's life is different; there is no universal definition of success and failure. None of us have any idea what really goes on inside the heads of others. We each need to live a life that works for us. But we should do it with dignity and respect for how others might be feeling. We can't change who we are. We can only be the best version of ourselves.

Once you stop comparing yourself with everybody else and just work on being the best you, a big load lifts. And when you get good at being you it's amazing how often you can lift those around you. I learnt from many years as a journalist that everybody is interesting, and everybody has a story. You just have to find it. It is worth pausing every so often and asking ourselves what our stories are. One thing I know for sure. Yours is unique.

Investing in the happiness of others

I wonder whether most of us really stop to consider what impact our words and actions have on others. I've lost count of the number of times I've seen shop assistants in tears because a customer was rude to them. I watch people charged with anger shaking their fists and abusing others on the road. We all get rude phone calls. People spend time trolling online with awful comments designed purely to bring others down.

All these actions just drag us all down. They take away the smiles and leaves holes in the heart. For really sensitive people, it can just destroy a whole day.

How much better would the world be if we used our special powers to influence the days of other people in a positive way? Every day you have the power to make someone else's day great or terrible. We should always choose great. It is our best and simplest contribution to a better world.

Being grateful

Lives can transform when we learn to be grateful for what we have and not regretful about things we don't. Everybody has something to be grateful for. Often, we take things for granted and don't take time to appreciate what we have or thank those who make our lives better.

American author Melody Beattie describes it in this way: "Gratitude unlocks the fullness of life. It turns what we have into enough, and more. It turns denial into acceptance, chaos to order, confusion to clarity. It can turn a meal into a feast, a house into a home, a stranger into a friend. Gratitude makes sense of our past, brings peace for today and creates a vision for tomorrow."

The more you see tragedy and pain in the world, the more you realise that a life where you have a roof over your head and enough to eat is a special gift. In fact, the mere fact of our existence is something of a miracle. Bill Bryson pointed out in his book *A Short History of Nearly Everything* that you could replay the entire genetic sequence that created humans and likely come up with a different form of life. And it would have only taken one fatal mishap in any of our long family histories for us not to exist as individuals. If not for accidents of geography our parents might never have met.

Life is not something to be taken for granted. Hey, you woke up today. Grab the day and be grateful for it. There is so much you can do with a day. What an amazing opportunity!

Walking away from bad relationships

Bad relationships just fill your life with toxin. If you believe the various research on the subject, an extraordinary number of people tolerate bad relationships in all aspects of their lives and often do nothing about it.

In the vast majority of cases, people later regret the life wastage this entails.

It seems obvious that life is too short to be dragged down by toxic people. Having the courage to recognise this and do something about it is a very different thing. For a whole lot of reasons people stay in violent domestic relationships, persevere with supervisors and managers who make their lives hell and spend time with people who always put them down. Inevitably the "nice" people become the victims and start making excuses for the toxic people who are contaminating their lives.

In the workplace, this is a difficult thing to manage. I've lost count of the number of times I've investigated allegations of "bullying" in the workplace where the HR conclusion is that there is no bullying under the legal or corporate conduct definition, the perpetrator is merely displaying a "sub-optimal" level of human behaviour. Or, as one person put it "there is no law against being a pain in the arse". Ultimately you cannot control the behaviour of others, only your own. Plenty of people waste enormous amounts of energy trying to change others. It sometimes works for a while. But most things in life and nature tend to return to a default point.

Having the courage to make change and cut loose from toxic people is a very personal thing. Most people cannot do it alone. They need a very strong support base to build up the courage, keep the courage and deal with the guilt that leaving any relationship brings. So, the first thing to do is build the support base. With that in place, the power and courage to change comes a lot easier.

Having a timetable for your dreams

Everybody has dreams. Everybody talks about what they will do "one day". Dreams, however, are just that. They are apparitions formed in our mind often based on a fantasy view of the world. Dreams only get fulfilled if they are in the plan and in the calendar.

We often mistake life for a medium-to-long-term flow of time in which plans form and are executed seamlessly and the things we want to do just float naturally into this continuum. This is fallacy. Life is actually a collection of individual days. Things can only happen if they form part of a day or a collection of days.

Once you face this reality, you quickly realise that you need an actual plan and timetable for your dreams. And, once you have that timetable, you need to put it in the calendar and on your schedule to make it happen. Whether it is visiting a particular overseas country, changing career, learning a language or taking a first aid course, you need to plan it. And you should do it now. Even if you are not going to do something for five years, if you have it in your forward calendar you will be working towards an activation point. That will vastly increase the chances of it happening and it will also give you a nice light on the horizon that will lift your mood.

Develop life-long fitness habits

There are thousands of books, websites and gurus devoted to telling you to do this. For good reason. If you get into good fitness and eating habits in your 20s and keep those habits for the rest of your life, you will have a better life in so many ways. You only have one body, and your older self will pay for what you do earlier in life.

I have good fitness habits now, but I didn't really start these until I was nearly 40. It was only then I realised that being fit felt so much better. You have more stamina for everything, your mind works better, and you still have endurance to do things after work at night.

It was not easy to get started. My only real discretionary time tends to be in the morning so I started allocating time then to get up to exercise. For the first year, I failed miserably. Too often my brain would wake up and say: "Why are we getting up at this ridiculous time, we need more sleep?" So, I would decide to start tomorrow. And then the day after that. And so on.

In the end I had to change the game. I decided to have coffee to wake me up before I went for a run. Instead of waking up to run, I woke up to have coffee. My brain was fine with that. "Mmmm," it would say. "It is definitely a good idea to get up and have coffee." Once I was awake and caffeinated a run seemed like a good use of time. It took about three weeks to genuinely form the habit and, many years later, I happily exercise every morning without even worrying about coffee.

Invest in family and friends

When it really matters, family and friends will be the people with you in the bunker. We know our family and friends will be there for us even if we neglect them a bit. That doesn't mean we should. If we don't constantly stop and ask ourselves what our true priorities are, we inevitably let the unrelenting rush of life and work override time with the people who matter most.

The realities of modern life mean it gets harder to invest genuine time in nurturing relationships. You really have to work at it. Most long-term studies of friendship show humans have about half as many close friends (as distinct from online friends) as they had a generation ago.

This is yet another example of our need to hyper-prioritise our options in life. It is always worth stopping for a while and asking which relationships are really important to us. Sometimes the answer is surprising.

Stop worrying about who gets the credit

United State President Harry S. Truman observed: "It is amazing what you can accomplish if you do not care who gets the credit." He was right. While it is always nice to get credit for your ideas and work, sometimes achieving the outcome is a lot more important than the kudos.

In particular, sharing ideas with people of influence can give those ideas a greater chance of becoming reality. If you sell an idea to someone and then they champion it to someone else, they suddenly have a vested interest in its success. It is always helpful to have a cheer squad when you are trying to get something across the line.

Stop sweating first-world problems

Talking about "first-world" problems has become a bit of a cliché. It is, however, useful to keep reminding ourselves that a lot of the things we spend time worrying about, are pretty minor in the scheme of things.

When you look at the sort of lives so many people in the world are consigned to, it highlights just how much we should be grateful for every day of healthy living. If you are alive, well fed, in work and you have close friends and a loving family you are in much better shape than the vast majority of people in history.

Similarly, there is very little evidence that chasing material possessions makes anybody happier. In fact, most of the evidence points to the opposite. We are only truly happy when we learn to appreciate what we have. Otherwise, our whole lives can become defined by an artificial failure or a frustrating sense that we are chasing dreams that will never happen.

Always give an honest, respectful opinion

I have found that the most influential people are the ones who always give an honest and respectful opinion. You can be fairly brutal in your assessments if they are made in a genuinely constructive way and you skillfully play the ball rather than the man or woman.

In his book *Good to Great*, Jim Collins outlines how the most successful companies develop a culture of robust feedback. If the culture is strong enough, such feedback can be delivered without causing offence. What's more, it overcomes the curse of silent disquiet that invades so many office cultures.

How often have you heard people say after a corporate failure that they knew a particular thing would not work but they did not say anything? This approach is of no use to anyone. If you build up a track record of respectful feedback, particularly where you have genuine expertise, your influence can grow tenfold.

Do not expect everything to be perfect, or even work

We spend a lot of time lamenting that the system sucks, that nothing works and that everything is too complicated or broken. This situation is not great, but it is also no surprise. We expect that things' working is the natural state. But if we fail to maintain, upgrade or fix things, then broken, derelict and overgrown is actually the default state.

Our whole world operates around fighting the natural state of brokenness. For everything to work all the time, we would need perfection. We will never have that. We should strive to make everything as good as it can possibly be. But, if it doesn't always work, we shouldn't be all that surprised. We just make the best of it and find someone who can fix it.

Default to constructive negotiation rather than conflict

This is true at a personal and global level. When something happens that cheeses us off – as a person, as a business, as a country – our natural reaction is usually to go into the bunker and fight. The truth is, in almost any situation, a reasoned and respectful discussion will resolve an issue or at least take it to a place where there is rational discussion without heat.

Parents used to tell children to count to 10 when they got angry. This was to give time to get out of the red zone and think rationally again. Imagine what a different world it would be if we defaulted to a positive resolution of issues rather than getting our backs up.

Learn to laugh

As they sang in Monty Python's *Life of Brian* – "life is quite absurd and that's the final word." There is no better way to transform a day than to laugh. I'm not sure any of us laugh enough these days. I think it is a great life tactic to proactively seek out people who make you laugh.

Mark Twain, the ultimate quote master, probably said it best: "Humanity has unquestionably one really effective weapon – laughter. Power, money, persuasion, supplication, persecution – these can lift at a colossal humbug – push it a little – weaken it a little, century by century. But only laughter can blow it to rags and atoms at a blast. Against the assault of laughter nothing can stand."

Great ideas are powerful, and cost you nothing

People are hungry for ideas and inspiration. The most influential people in the world are not afraid to float ideas. When they do, people around them light up, cluster around the ideas and go off and make magic. Never be afraid to champion a good idea.

Things work best with people you like and trust

If you attend enough conferences and business speeches, after a while they all start to sound the same. But then occasionally somebody says something unexpected. At one such event, the CEO of a very successful company was asked to name the one thing that made his business successful. His answer was that he only did business with people he liked. What the? Surely that was not possible. Could anybody really be that choosy in a tough economy?

I've asked a lot of people about this notion over the years. Few have gone to the extreme of banning people they do not like but plenty believe their most profitable business was done with people they liked. This was partly because there was better collaboration and sharing of ideas.

When you do business with difficult or toxic people all the time, it is draining. Great firms seem to have a knack of finding people that they love doing business with. And everyone basks in, and celebrates, the mutual success.

It is the same with hobbies and almost anything else we do in life. Our passions are even more powerful shared with great people.

7. Simple ways to better days

Years ago, I was listening to a radio interview with a man who was about to retire after 40 years in the same job. That was his only newsworthiness. The interviewer was just interested in why someone would spend so long with the same employer. I guess that is becoming rare. In many respects, he was an unremarkable man. He enjoyed routine. He worked to live and he made the most of his job without it being the dominant part of his life.

Then the interviewer asked him how he coped with the inevitable tough days and the baggage that comes with staying at one place for so long, his answer was simple. He kept a message prominently on his desk that simply said: "There are always better days."

Whenever the man was having a bad day, he just looked at the message, shrugged his shoulders and thought ahead to a point when today's little drama would be in the past.

For some reason this simple piece of advice has always stuck with me. It is so true. We have good days and bad days. No matter how many bad days you have, there will

always be good ones ahead. Time, even a single day, is a great cleanser.

I find it really useful to "life cleanse" at the start of every year. The great thing about the Christmas and New Year period is that it gives us a good excuse to hit the reboot button. It is like waking up to a new dew-lustred day. The opportunities look fresh, and renewal has a context.

I've always been a big believer in New Year resolutions. I make them every year, strictly limit the number and constantly refer back to them. In general, I keep at least 60% of the commitments and I'm fairly happy with that result.

The following are a few of my New Year ideas that have proven useful over time:

Create 10 memorable days

Humans live an average of about 30,000 days but the reality is we remember details of only a very small number. These tend to be the defining days – some positive, some negative.

The good news is we can create positive, memorable days each year if we set out pro-actively to do it. This could include buying tickets to special concerts or events, arranging a social event, trying something new and challenging, arranging to meet somebody interesting or going on a ground-breaking holiday. These memorable days can be the difference between a watershed year and one that barely registers in the retention banks.

Prioritise sleep

This may seem like a simple thing, but it is vital. The old adage says you are what you eat. You could equally say you are how you sleep. There is a mountain of evidence suggesting that adequate, quality sleep is one of the key components to a happy, healthy and successful life. There is equally powerful evidence that a disturbing number of people are sacrificing sleep due to work and life demands – too many options, too little time.

Even people who do spend enough time in bed often don't make it to the quality, deep sleep required for general body maintenance and rejuvenation. Sleep deprivation eats off our edges slowly. Our mood and effectiveness deteriorate, our decision-making suffers, and our wellbeing is chipped away like an invisible, creeping malaise.

Many people boast they can survive on just a few hours of sleep. There is a big difference between surviving and quality living.

Change any bad habits from the first week

We all have work habits we know are bringing us down – bad email practices, too many meetings, getting into routines that entail working too many hours etc. The start of the year is the best time to fix one or all of these. If you start the year with the same bad habits, it never seems like the right time to fix them. Just after New Year feels like the perfect time.

Plan all of your breaks for the year

Peace of mind and contentment can be strongly linked to having something to look forward to. If you have the post-Christmas work blues, keep yourself motivated by planning what you will do at Easter or how you will spend your annual leave time – and book it in. Even the worst days seem better when you have something relaxing to look forward to.

Lock in a new activity

John Lennon famously wrote that life is what happens to you while you are busy making other plans. Most of us have activities – sport, hobbies etc – which we really enjoy but our busy jobs don't allow us to do.

If we are honest, this is really a prioritisation issue. We are consciously de-prioritising things that make us happy. The best way to counter this is to commit to something at the beginning of the year in a way that obligates you to prioritise – pay the money to do it upfront, arrange to do it with people you don't want to let down and pro-actively plan your work schedule around it.

One of the best places to start is revisiting the things we enjoyed when we were younger and had fewer commitments. It is amazing how often we stop doing our most cherished childhood activities by the time we are in our early 20s. How many people stick with organised sport into their 30s for example?

Avoid screens for at least two hours before you sleep

Many of us have become addicted to the constant flow of emails, communications, and social media posts on our smartphones. As a result, we are always "on" and our sleep and general wellbeing are undermined by a bombardment of electronic impulses that stimulate our brains at a time when we should be moving into dormant mode. Ignoring the phone and reading a good, old-fashioned book before sleep can be life changing.

Lock in a de-clutter day

Even the messiest of people can feel weighed down by clutter. If we are overwhelmed by "stuff", it creates a feeling that things are out of control. Proactively setting aside a few hours to clean up an office or home and create a decent filing system (paper or electronic) can create a great feeling of empowerment. Order gives us the clear air we need to think and sends a potent message of enablement and contentment.

8. Getting through really tough days

We all know about THOSE days. You feel a bit off. You make a big mistake. Someone is filling your world with toxin and then a customer phones you to offer some helpful abuse for a problem that you have no control over.

Add to the mix the need to deliver some bad news, a crisis of confidence, a deadline you can't reach without forfeiting sleep and your desperately needed gym session, and you are seriously messing with your inner consonance.

On the flipside, as Roman poet Horace said, adversity "has the effect of eliciting talents which in prosperous circumstances would have lain dormant". It just never feels like it at the time and in the middle of a crisis the last thing you would want is Horace prancing around in his robes reciting poetry.

Anyone who thinks they can have a completely hassle-free life is delusional. It is far better to just expect the rough days and be ready to go to your *Dealing with a Bad Day Plan* as soon as you realise one is upon you. Here are some thoughts on how to deal with bad days.

Talk to your biggest fan

Almost everyone has someone in their lives that they know will always be on their side, no matter what – a spouse, partner, friend, parent, sibling, mentor, or really supportive work colleague – whoever it is. On the days when you are struggling you need to call them or see them, and just vent. Getting things off your chest to someone who knows that you are great will release the pressure and give you perspective. They will not mind. They are your biggest fan after all. That's why you have each other. You would do the same for them.

Don't bottle it up and don't try to handle it alone. Humans are social creatures and getting the agro out is far healthier than boxing it in. Once you let it out, your brain starts functioning properly again and perspective returns.

Absurdification

I sometimes call this Fawlty Towering a day, in honour of the superb John Cleese comedy *Fawlty Towers*. If you allow yourself, you can find satire and absurdity in even the toughest circumstances. We need to take important things seriously but most of what happens in our days is not far from a seriously funny sitcom script. If you set out to absurdify a tense situation you might realise just how laughable the whole thing is. If you do it right, you can quickly go from high stress to barely holding back the guffaws.

I probably should not admit this, but the first time I got out of journalism, quite a few years ago, I worked for a government department and had to write media releases for the first time. In the beginning the spin and the things bureaucrats actually said (think *Yes Minister*) just messed with my head. Most journalists who have made the conversion will know what I mean. Eventually, as a form of conversion therapy, I would write the real media statement and then write another satirical version after work, without the spin, just for my own amusement. From that, I found I could deal with any circumstance without stress.

When I went back into media, the alternative, satirical media releases evolved into a column I wrote for a couple of publications. Then I applied the approach to all of human life in the book *Tall People Don't Jump*. I'm not suggesting for a minute that we treat the serious stuff flippantly. But framing a bad day in satirical terms can be a tonic. (And, yes, I know absurdification is not an actual word. Yet).

Be in control of how you react to the situation

Much has been written about the insights of the great Holocaust survivor Viktor Frankl and his concept of the last human freedom – our ability to decide how we will react to any situation (see Page 142). Only we control this. Yet so often we just let others control it for us. It is easier said than done, but you can give yourself permission not to react negatively to situations imposed on you by others. As soon as we let someone stress us through bad behaviours or attitudes, we give their behaviour credibility and access to our precious emotional core. Why? Inside your head is all yours. You can decide whom you let in there.

How bad is it really?

When I'm having a bad day at work, I Google Malala Yousafzai and apply the Malala test to my day. Malala is an inspirational young Pakistani woman shot by the Taliban for having the audacity to campaign for the rights of young women to education. She survived – barely. And when she was well enough she started campaigning again. When you read stories about people who have really suffered, and then you look at the first world "crisis" you are having at work it is easy to then ask yourself: "How bad is my problem really?"

Turn your emphasis to after work

Bad days actually end. When they do it is probably a good idea not to just go home and fret and burn a night's sleep.

These are the days when you need something to look forward to – something fun and distracting. As soon as you know there is a bad day upon you, you need to get your mindset into a spot beyond the working environment, with people who will brighten your soul. Plan it and lock it in. Do something spontaneous and know that beyond the dark clouds is some guaranteed sunshine. The default position in life is generally on the sunny side, thankfully.

Outsource your worry

I always say to anyone reporting to me that if they are making a decision that will cause them to lose sleep, they need to tell me about it that day. If I support the decision, I'm happy to take responsibility for it and relieve them of any reason to worry. Some people will worry anyway, but this approach seems to help in a lot of cases. Sharing a burden or outsourcing up the chain to give you peace of mind can do wonders for your sleep.

Treasure your complaints

This is hard to do but it can be extremely energising to always set out to turn your mistakes into a positive. Journalists will tell you that their best contacts often come from stories where they made a mistake but made the effort to fix it and really understand the gripe.

Australian hairdressing entrepreneur Stefan Ackerie runs his empire with a mantra of "treasure your complaints". When his company becomes aware of grievances, they deal with them urgently, quickly make amends and ensure everyone involved learns from the experience. As a result, their complainants become their most valuable word of mouth advocates.

The natural human reaction is generally to hide a mistake and become defensive. You will have a better day if you admit it and try to turn it into a positive for the future. This from American human rights activist Malcolm X: "Every defeat, every heartbreak, every loss contains its own seed, its own lesson on how to improve your performance next time." We are only human. If we were perfect, we would be boring.

Return to an awe moment

Golfer Greg Norman used to talk about the rare days when he was in awe of himself – every shot went right; every bit of luck went his way – he could do no wrong. We all have awe moments from time to time, occasions when we totally nail something – a presentation goes just right, our tennis serve finds the groove, or we get a job against the odds.

There is a great technique taught in leadership courses to capture those moments. Spend a full 10 minutes with your eyes shut imagining a very slow walk through a well-known and favourite place. At the end of the 10 minutes put two fingers together really hard and concentrate with all of your mind energy on the most euphoric moment of your life. If you really surrender to the process, you can squeeze your fingers together any time in the weeks and months that follow and feel the euphoria run through you.

I don't know the psychology behind it, but it works. And it can be very handy on tough days or if you are about to do something you are dreading.

Tackling a confidence crisis

Author Marianne Williamson speculated: "Our deepest fear is not that we are inadequate. Our deepest fear is that we are powerful beyond measure. It is our light, not our darkness that most frightens us." In an episode of *The West Wing* television program, during a really bad day press secretary C.J. Cregg wonders wistfully if the people running the White House are really the best the United States can do in making such big decisions.

Crises of confidence are normal. On some level many people think they are frauds – doing their best, making it up as they go along, hoping to make enough good decisions to hide the fact that they don't have all the answers. I'm totally sure that most new American presidents have a moment of panic when they realise they are actually in charge of the security of the free world.

Never think you are unusual if you have a day in which you just don't feel up to the job – people are relying on you, but you feel like you are letting them down. Take heart from the fact that you wouldn't be in the job if somebody didn't think you were up to it. And your call on most things will be as good as anybody else's. We are storing intuition from the day we are born. Just having lived makes you qualified to make a reasonable call in at least 90 per cent of situations.

Go counterintuitive

Everyone tends to learn the hard way that you can almost never control someone else's behaviour, no matter how bad it is. But you can control yours. Sometimes dealing with a bad day imposed by a toxic colleague requires totally counterintuitive behaviour – what author and researcher Shawn Achor would call changing the social script.

If someone says something patronising, condescending or negative most people's instinct is to get upset and even demand redress. The other option is to rewrite the script in a positive dialogue. Send a note thanking them for their feedback and asking their opinion on another matter. In fact, making a point of regularly seeking input from colleagues who seem to have a problem with you can quickly change the whole dynamic.

Often the bile has come from the fact that the toxic person feels threatened by you or believes that their experience and input is not valued. As soon as you demonstrate that you value them, their attitude can quickly change. I've seen people become genuine friends this way, once they start to fully understand each other. I would never condone bad behaviour but sometimes you just have to go with the things you can control.

Embrace the learnings

Living is a tremendous privilege and having a good job and regular income remains just a pipe dream for millions around the world. Bad days are part of the fabric of being lucky enough to live a corporate life and vital to our personal growth and coping skills. Most of the time nobody dies or gets hurt. When you have a bad day, there is no point in acting surprised. People have been having them for centuries. If you expect them, keep the problems in perspective and have a well-rehearsed plan for dealing with them, they are not so scary.

Power up and power down your day

The start of the day is important. It can set the tone for the whole day. I find it is always better to have 30 minutes at the beginning of every day to get some broader context before I start any real work.

I spend this time reading news and opinions from around the world, consuming a couple of interesting business or social science articles and sending emails to people who I want to keep in touch with or consult on something. This kick-starts and calibrates my brain. I always have more productive days when I start like this.

Similarly, it really helps to power down your day. This means finding some time at the end of the day to round off your to-do list, carry things that haven't been done to the next day's list and give yourself a sense of completeness. Tomorrow is another day. You are much more likely to sleep properly and feel balanced if you can compartmentalise your day, and physically and mentally shut the door on your workday.

Keep a notebook full of great ideas and wisdom

Like many people, I often go to inspiring presentations, read books that have incredible insights and just hear interesting quotes or words of wisdom during my day.

For years most of these gave me a moment of reflection and then just floated by. Some time ago I realised this was a waste. So I went retro and started writing them down in a journal.

I do this every time I hear a presentation or hear or read something I want to remember. For most books I read, there are about five insights I want to hold onto. I write them down in the journal, so they are always in one place. Now I use that journal when I need inspiration, but it also feeds conversations and provides useful material and stories for my own presentations. Flipping through my ideas journal never fails to lift me on days when I feel flat.

Have three lists on your desk

For years I struggled with my daily to-do list. It didn't work. There were usually 20 things on it and most days, once you factored meetings in, about four things got done.

I got sick of every day feeling like a failure. So I went to three lists. The first is my "today" list. It usually has about four things on it and I nearly always get four things done.

My second list is my "discussion list" which has the names of management peers and direct reports and the things I need to discuss with them. This allows me to park things neatly as they arise and be ready to discuss them at the appropriate meeting.

List three is my medium-term priorities. This has about eight things that I want to achieve or make progress on over the course of the year. Sometimes aspects of these go onto my "today" list but the full list is always on my desk so I don't lose sight of bigger picture strategic needs in the humdrum of the everyday. Generally, I only need to update this list a few times a year.

There was a time when three lists would have seemed excessive and inefficient. Now it makes me feel in control of my day and empowered to achieve.

9. Living a life of no regrets

Various people are credited with the simple proposition that a happy life for almost everybody comes down to three simple things – having something worthwhile to do, having someone to love and having something to look forward to. As a basic philosophy, this is not a bad starting point. Here are a few others I would add.

Be true to yourself

This seems to be a simple and self-evident reality, but the facts suggest it remains elusive for a tragic proportion of the population. Hospice nurse Bronnie Ware wrote a remarkable book (*The Top Five Regrets of the Dying*) exploring the most common regrets of patients who knew they were going to die. Top of the regrets list was not having the courage to live a life that was true to yourself rather than the life that was expected of you.

How often do you hear of people "settling", compromising, and finding every excuse to avoid an inner voice reminding them that they are fundamentally unhappy with their lives, their jobs and the ways they spend their days?

We are all victims of the curse of the everyday. We get up every morning, we live busy lives and then we go to sleep. It is so easy to do this for hundreds, even thousands of days without any self-disruption. This inertia can consume our lives and sabotage our efforts to find the "one thing" mentioned earlier in this book.

The other big regrets in Ware's book were: Working too hard, failing to stay in touch with friends, having the courage to express feelings to people who were important to us and just not allowing ourselves to be happy.

Fast forward 30 years. How many of us will have pretty much the same list? What are we going to do about it this year?

Do not accept the stress imposed by others

I am always astounded at the willingness of people to let others impose stress on them. The one thing nobody else can control is the way we feel inside our own heads. We are totally empowered to decide that nobody will get us down. Yet, we let them in. Why?

When you allow yourself to become upset or stressed by someone, by definition you are giving their behaviour credence, giving them access to your precious emotional centre and giving them some control of your life. Why?

Austrian neurologist Viktor Frankl famously survived the Nazi concentration camps by refusing to allow the Nazi's to control his inner mind. In *Man's Search for Meaning*, he offers one of the most profound lines ever written about the human condition: "Everything can be taken from a man but one thing: the last of the human freedoms – to choose one's attitude in any given set of circumstances, to choose one's own way."

Frankl also believed that pursuing success and happiness was fruitless. He contended that both could only be achieved as an "unintended side-effect" of a cause greater than one's self or as a by-product of surrendering ourselves fully to somebody else.

A more recent study of 1200 elderly people, known as the Legacy Project, also asked the research group to articulate their main regret. Far and away the main response was worrying. If people had their time over they would spend less of it on empty concerns about things that almost never eventuated.

I have generally been lucky in the stress department. Most of the time the only stress I allow into my emotional centre is from people I respect or care about – because that stress is meaningful and requires action. The rest I generally find absurd, and sometimes hilarious: "Nice try but the inside of my head is mine, thank-you very much."

Chase days that energise

One of my favourite episodes of *The West Wing* includes a scene where President Bartlett laments that he wants to have more days where he feels better at the end of the day than the start of the day. Ever since I first saw that episode some years ago, it has been my yardstick on whether I am doing the right job and spending my days doing the right thing.

Let's face it, if our days drain us rather than energise us, we are almost certainly doing the wrong thing and we have clearly not found the "one thing" that will enrich our lives.

Learn to live without fear

This is easier said than done, but it is another common trait among those who claim to be content. Some fear is necessary to stop us doing really stupid things. But an incredible number of people live their lives constantly obsessed with what might go wrong. There is a famous social experiment in which a group of surfers are being trained on a beach that has rocks. If the instructor constantly warns them not to surf towards the rocks, a large proportion of them end up on the rocks. If the rocks are never mentioned, most of the surfers just go safely to the beach. Concentrating on things that can go wrong just increases the risk of that happening and creates artificial stress.

Embracing luck and opportunity

I spent Christmas Eve a few years ago in the town of Albert in northern France where there are thousands of graves of young Australians who died on the battlefields of World War I. As I walked the lonely and desolate fields, I imagined a generation fuelled with hope only to have their lives extinguished so far from home and in such horrendous circumstances.

It occurred to me that those of us blessed with a life without chronic pain and enriched with opportunity and the freedom to choose our own path, owed it to these young men not to squander what we have been given. The gift of existence is often taken for granted and is so frequently compromised for reasons that clearly appear lame to those who lie in hospices contemplating a life that might have been.

It could be one thing. If we are born lucky, it could be a tapestry of things that we pursue as homage to the privilege of being. We really do have much to be grateful for.

10. Learning to believe in yourself

The great John Lennon observed in 1970 that "there ain't no guru who can see through your eyes". It was a remarkably astute, yet simple observation. None of us really know what goes on in anybody else's head. And there is a fair chance any assumptions we make will be wrong.

This is particularly so with self-confidence. For years I just assumed most people were confident and self-assured. It took a long time to realise just how many people struggle with self-belief. Often these are the best-performing people.

The trouble is most of us do not really know how we are perceived by others (unless someone we trust actually takes the time to tell us). None of us really know whether the reaction of our brain to a task is the same as the reaction of others. If you read the biographies of the world's great achievers, almost all of them have times when they doubt their abilities and feel like a fraud in whatever they are doing.

Renowned American author John Steinbeck was one. "I am not a writer," he said in 1938. "I've been fooling myself and other people." There are similar reflections in the public realm from John F Kennedy, Abraham Lincoln, Robbie Williams, Steven Spielberg and even the great Leonardo da Vinci (who questioned whether he had contributed anything of value to the world). These are just a few of the hundreds of similar examples.

Self-belief is such a personal thing, and we are all wired differently. But, based on my observations of people who have overcome chronic self-doubt, the following are a few things you might try.

Develop a super-confidence mode

This is just a mindset thing. If you learn to psyche yourself into a highly confident mode it can work remarkably well. Even just saying "I'm going to totally nail this" over and over in your head can move your mind to a state of positivity. You just have to do it proactively, particularly if you find yourself drifting into doubt. It is hard to just chip away at doubt. It is much easier to try to blast it away.

Do not compare yourself to anybody else

Most people fall into the trap of always comparing themselves with others. And plenty of people are really hard on themselves. You can only ever be as good as you can be. It is pointless comparing yourself to the performance or methods of someone else. Great athletes can have completely different styles but still produce similar level performances. It is okay to have your own way of doing things. There are many different ways to approach a task. You just need to find the way that works for you.

Do not wait for feedback

If you are doubting your abilities, just ask your boss, supervisor or a peer to give you some honest feedback on how you are performing and how you are perceived. Most people will tell you and be quite happy to. You might be surprised how positively you are perceived by others. And when they tell you, you will feel your confidence soar.

In fact, while you are at it, why don't you just tell somebody else what a great job they are doing? You can pretty much guarantee that plenty of people sitting around you are doubting their abilities. You can easily make their day with a bit of positive, honest feedback.

11. Giving yourself permission to rest

In your teens and twenties, you get a false impression that you can be on the go all day and all night and your body will just bounce back. The older you get, the slower the bounce back. To have a sustainable life, you need to properly rest in between sprints.

There is a mountain of clear evidence that we all work much more effectively when we give our bodies proper recovery time.

The book *Rest* by Alex Soojung-Kim Pang is a treasure trove of examples from history of how the great achievers used rest as a secret weapon to achieve greatness.

I was particularly struck by the idea that great writers learned to stop work while they were on a roll. This allowed them to pick up at the next session where they left off with no loss of momentum or creative nourishment. As Ernest Hemmingway put it: "Always stop when you are going good and don't think about it or worry about it until you start to write the next day. That way your subconscious will work on it all the time. But if you think about it consciously or worry about it you will kill it and your brain will be tired before you start." This approach runs counter to how most of us work. We tend to keep going when we are on a roll, fearing that if we stop we will lose our mojo. Since I read the Pang book, I have made a big effort to change my habits. And it works.

That book also cites a multitude of research projects and

case studies that back the view that humans have a declining marginal return from the hours worked. Long hours seldom equate to better or even a higher volume of quality work outcomes.

Even when faced with compelling research, many of us struggle to prioritise rest time. Personally, any time I spend resting tends to be accompanied with a feeling of guilt. I think this comes from a busy life – working hard, raising kids, trying to keep a house maintained and functional and never, ever running out of things to do.

The things we need to do just keep staring at us and willing us to get off the bed or the couch and do something. Increasingly I have realised that rest can't be the opposite of doing something. It has to be an important something in itself.

Whenever I speak to my father, he always observes that I seem to be doing too much and I need to make time to have a "spell". I love the word spell. My Dad has been using it my whole life. I gather the word had its origins in meaning people did a spell at something, as in they did their turn doing something. The meaning eventually morphed into a spell also being time spent resting.

Dad worked hard in manual jobs for all his working life and well knew that you couldn't just keep physically exerting yourself without some respite from time to time. This is less obvious in knowledge jobs using our brains. We can be wearing ourselves out in our heads, but it does not manifest the same as when we do physical work. By the time we get to what many of us term "mentally tired" we have probably pushed well past a place where our brains are working well.

Whenever I write about this subject, I find a large amount of the response comes from people in the finance and legal industries, particularly young people who are finding their days are fully dominated by work.

It feels like the emerging generation of young workers are caught in a quandary between getting ahead quickly and feeling that their lives are out of balance. I get countless emails from people who feel trapped in a working life that leaves them feeling empty.

There is no simple answer. Ultimately, we all have to decide how we will prioritise our time and whether we will control our lives or let others control them for us. We all need to ask what really matters and what is really achieved by working too hard and never resting.

When I talk to people who believe that have a balanced life, the common thread seems to be that they lock in time for rest and recreation. It is their highest priority rather than something they just do if there is any time left in the day. That is a good start.

12. Giving yourself permission to be happy

Happy is an odd sort of word. There is nothing sophisticated about it. It has a couple of syllables, and it spells like it sounds. It will not earn you too many points in scrabble and you seldom find it in a crossword puzzle.

Despite the simplicity of the word, it represents one of the most fundamental aspirations of humans and is one of the most complex notions that we contend with in our daily lives.

We all want to be happy.

That should be simple. However, it inevitably becomes difficult when we try to define what happiness is for each of us.

Is it our daily mindset? Is it something we aspire to in the future? Is it some sort of residual measurement we end up with when we do a ledger of everything we do in our lives?

The most likely answer is that happiness is different for everyone. We all know people who we believe to be happy based on a broad, general definition.

Generally, these people have a mix of the following characteristics:

- They have a positive attitude to life most of the time
- They don't let setbacks get them down too much
- They enjoy how they spend their days
- Their lives are filled with positive relationships and people who support them

This seems simple enough. Surely if we all just do that; we should all be happy all of the time.

If only humans were so uncomplicated.

In truth, a large chunk of the population does not have a positive attitude to life. In fact, in many situations, if you start talking negatively about something, fairly quickly you can find a chorus of supporters positively reveling in talking things down. Many people absolutely thrive on negativity.

Despite our best efforts to avoid stress and not let things get us down, our Negative Nelly brains work hard at giving us things to worry about. It is a constant internal battle to keep Nelly in her place.

Lots of people enjoy what they do during their days. I suspect lots more roll out of bed each day dreading the hours ahead – work, running children around, doing the washing, making meals – all of the routines that are required to meet our needs, wants and sense of civility and order.

Those of us lucky enough to be in good relationships and part of supportive communities have a definite advantage in the quest for happiness. Sadly, way too many people are in bad relationships and lack a strong network of friends or genuine community involvement.

In short, even though we all aspire to happiness, a scary number of people look in the mirror each morning to see someone struggling to find their smile. I have reflected on this a lot over the years and one conclusion always bubbles to the surface – we can only be happy if we give ourselves permission to be happy.

If I am being honest with myself, I personally struggle to give myself this permission. In fact, I regularly lapse into an illogical belief that as soon as I allow myself to be happy, something bad will happen. I am amazed when I speak candidly about this to other people, how many others are loaded down with the same affliction.

This is a particularly dumb way to approach life and sits with the same syndrome that causes us to worry about all sorts of things that might happen even when the odds are low. For example, we can spend all day worrying about an asteroid striking Earth. Or we can just deal with what is actually happening and ignore the things that might happen.

Those of a certain religious ilk talk about "Catholic Guilt", which has evolved to mean a deep feeling of guilt that people feel all the time, even when there is little to be logically guilty about.

When I self-reflect, I suspect I am at my happiest when I take the time to feel grateful, I spend time with people who genuinely care about me and I am working on projects in my day that I cannot wait to get stuck into.

I am least happy when I feel overwhelmed by my to-do list, I spend too much time with people who drain me, and my day is mostly made up of things that bore me witless.

When you strip it down to these types of basics, the conversion from unhappy to happy is relatively simple and requires relatively small changes to your day, or your life.

Giving yourself permission to be happy is harder. Sometimes it requires a massive mental shift from lamenting your circumstances to embracing them and concentrating on the things you are grateful for.

It also requires us to suspend worry about negative things that will happen in the future (aging, death, financial setbacks etc) and living in the positive aspects of today.

Often it requires even more than that. You might need to leave a toxic long-term relationship, find a better job or push yourself out of your comfort zone.

As I get older, I am increasingly of the view that happiness is not something we should "pursue". Happiness has to be a state that we live in. Now. All the time.

That does not mean we all should be deliriously happy every minute of every day. It just means that we should have a base disposition towards finding the positives in life.

I believe it is also important to regularly self-analyse what really makes us happy and fight hard to do more of that and put it at the core of our lives.

Ultimately, I think we are most valuable to ourselves and others around us when we finally say it is okay to want to be happy and to prioritise the things that make us feel good about life.

If you think about it, any other approach to life does not make a lot of sense.

13. Overcoming the curse of busyness

Contemporary society has developed an unhealthy obsession with busyness. Sometimes it feels like we wear it as a badge of honour.

It is as if our social and professional kudos requires a celebration of how full our lives are and our existence is not complete without committing to a frenetic life pace.

In our everyday encounters, conversations quickly turn to how busy we all are. Too much to do, so little time. Always running. Always due somewhere.

The trend is dangerous. Too often busyness is equated with stress, unhealthy habits, a feeling of failure and a foreboding sense that our lives are out of control. That is no way to live.

Every so often we need to take stock and proactively take back control of our time.

Here are some thoughts on how.

Recognise that busyness is largely a myth

It is simple maths. There are only 24 hours in the day, and you are doing something for every one of those hours – sleeping, working, parenting, playing, whatever it is.

You cannot possibly be busier than you were yesterday, last week or last year. Recognising that is the first step to getting out of the busyness trap.

If you feel busy it inevitable means you are trying to do too much with your limited time. That is where you need to start. What can I realistically do today? You can't add time. You can only use what is there.

You need to get real about what you can achieve and take the other stuff off the list or carry it forward. Otherwise every day feels like a failure. Nobody wants that.

Diarise time to do things

While this might seem obvious, lots of people have a long to-do list but don't allocate time to do the things on it. They diarise meetings but don't include time to do other work or the other things they need for their lives to function.

Time is precious and limited. If it is allocated for the things that most matter, you can take back control and really think about priorities – both work and private. If you only have time to work and no time to live, Houston we have a problem.

Two-pace work

This is also known as bunching chores. People typically have a long list of things to do and work through them in random order. Some things take quite a while, others a few minutes.

If you cluster the things that only take a few minutes into a "super hour", where you do those and nothing else, it is astounding how much you can get through. It is also satisfying to be crossing lots off the to-do list in quick time.

Allocate time to do nothing

As discussed in the previous chapter, we aren't machines. We can only do our work successfully if we have the brain space and the physical energy to do it.

It is important to allocate time to rest at the times when you are most busy. Putting rest time in your diary is really empowering. It allows you to find some space and give your brain some free capacity to do things properly.

On his death bed in 2017, 1970s pop icon David Cassidy is reported to have said "so much wasted time". It is a common lament.

Once we truly recognise the gift of time and take control of how we use it, our lives suddenly feel more enriched and under control. That is a way to live.

14. Freeing yourself from the competition

When I was young, I was highly competitive. All the time. I liked to win and be the best. My swim coach told me I spent too much time looking at where the other swimmers were when I was racing. He said I needed to swim my own race. Running was a similar story. I would look sideways near the line, and often get passed.

It was a bit the same when I started work. I was constantly concerned I wasn't advancing fast enough and I would worry about why someone younger than me was in a more senior job.

Then time happened.

Over the years you start to realise that a career advancement hierarchy is largely a myth. You go up, you go sideways, you go down. It really doesn't matter. There are also no really meaningful comparable levels between people and jobs across organisations. Plenty of great people are leaders without titles. Plenty of happy people do the same job for 20 years and love it.

There is no definition of success. You get to make up your own.

More importantly, your career has no logical nexus with anyone else's career. It is yours. As long as you get out of bed and look forward to your day, you are in pretty good shape. The only pressure comes from yourself. And you have total power to remove it.

These days when I swim I just cruise along in my lane at a pace that feels comfortable. It was such a great feeling to set myself free from the other lanes.

SECTION 4

Riding the waves of change

"The greatest discovery of all time is that a person can change his future by merely changing his attitude."
- **Oprah Winfrey** (talk show host, actress and author)

1. The forces reshaping our working lives

Change is not new. It always happens. Human existence has evolved from simple creatures with subsistence lives to complex societies using technologies that once existed only in science fiction.

Sometimes we act like change is something new. Many aspects of life may well be changing more quickly than in the past. But, keep in mind, not all that long ago streetlights were powered by whale oil and trains were powered by steam.

Humans are resilient to change. We just need to ride with the changes that are happening in our own lifetime and try to see change as an opportunity rather than a problem.

A few years ago, a few companies (Netflix among them) caused a sensation when they announced they were giving staff unlimited holidays. Entrepreneur Richard Branson picked up on the idea and has been an advocate for some time.

"What the?" was most people's first reaction, "You can't run a business like that." Maybe you can.

The move is not about staff being away on leave all the time. Branson and others were working on the same principle as an all-you-can-eat restaurant. Just because you can have 10 courses does not mean you do. But the possibility gives you options and empowerment.

Branson's typically lateral approach to staff motivation may well be seen in the future as a tipping point for our whole notion of work, life prioritisation and employment as an economic entity.

Clearly there is a groundswell of impending revolution in the worker ranks, particularly among the emerging generations, against the post-industrial age 9am to 5pm employment mindset that has morphed to a 7am to 7pm or "always-work-connected" mindset for large numbers of employees. This is just one of the seismic forces shaking up everything we have grown up to believe about work, careers and business. Here are some more.

A fundamental reshaping of available jobs

A 2013 study from the Oxford Martin School caused quite a stir when it concluded that technology would make 45% of jobs in the United States vulnerable to extinction in the following 20 years (although a separate OECD study put the figure at around a third of that, and a more recent McKinsey Global Institute report predicted 375 million jobs were likely to substantially disappear over the next decade due to the adoption of Artificial Intelligence). Regardless of the real number, it is becoming obvious that jobs that can be done by computers or robots probably will be in the not-too-distant future.

This is not necessarily a bad thing if it saves humans from dangerous and monotonous roles, and economies have been remarkably resilient at adapting to these forces in the past. However, the workforce will always have unskilled or poorly educated labour. Our biggest challenge comes in finding new avenues for that labour. If we don't, we will have vastly divergent classes of workers and chronic, socially damaging structural unemployment. That will be one of our biggest challenges over the next two decades.

I suspect the answer will lie in creating new bridges between technical work and high-tech work. There are some positive signs in this area. For example, some companies who have moved from manually welding lines in their factories to robotics have found that the human welders are best placed to drive the robots. The welders fundamentally understand the task to be done. These types of transitions will require some creative and lateral thinking from employers. The opportunity is there to be had if we embrace it.

The rise of the micro-business

While large numbers of countries have long relied on tiny businesses as the basis of their economy, in many western countries this has been less prevalent.

The Millennial generation is changing all that. Increasing numbers of young people are more interested in working for themselves at a young age rather than a boss or a corporation. I hear constant stories about young people who studied a traditional degree but found they could not cope with the culture of a traditional workplace. In a world where the Internet opens everyone to global markets, this trend is only likely to grow.

Up until very recently, typical start-up entrepreneurs in Australia have been aged in their thirties whilst those in Silicon Valley have been in their twenties. The Australian situation will almost inevitably change as the next generation feels more comfortable living in the "Baby Boomer Headquarters" family home and trying some business ideas early in life without too many overheads or risks.

This could be a good thing. The make-your-own-job entrepreneur makes a lot of sense in a world that is disrupting quickly and in which many big businesses struggle to maintain the overheads of scale in a shifting sands industrial landscape.

Enterprise clustering

Further to this, I have noticed in recent years a greater clustering of micro-businesses to tackle bigger jobs. These clusters can form (like when the Planeteers combine to form Captain Planet in the cartoon series) and then go back to their individual size when the big job is done. This seems like a very efficient economic structure.

Redundancy as a class of employment

There was a time when redundancy was something that might have happened once, maybe twice, in a lifetime when you were in the wrong place at the wrong time. Now it has emerged as a new class of between-jobs "employment". Most of us know at least a handful of people living on a large redundancy payment while they retrain and plan their next move. They are neither unemployed, nor in the workforce.

This raises some interesting questions. How much corporate dead money is being ploughed into structural adjustment around redundancy, and is that really sustainable? Do we need to totally rethink our industrial structures to recognise that change is constant and all-pervasive? Do we just need more flexible and fast-moving employment and organisational structures to allow companies to staff up and down but still give people employment certainty? The micro-companies may well be a manifestation of that.

The retirement numbers do not add up

Australian demographer Bernard Salt talks about the "demographic fault line". This refers to the historical phase we have entered in which large numbers of baby boomers are entering retirement age; while the feeder population of young people has dropped due to lower birth numbers in the 80s when the female workforce participation rate was rising. The result is a much lower net increase in the number of working age people each year.

To continue to drive economic growth, and fill skilled jobs, there will be little choice but for older workers to stay in the workforce longer, or to top up the working age population through migration. At the same time, meeting the retirement income needs of an ageing population remains a scary proposition over coming decades. While nobody would want any worker to stay in the workforce beyond their physical capabilities, everything points to the need for people who are capable of working for longer to do so and for the next generation to abandon the idea of a pension at 65. We will clearly need to lift financial self-dependency for long-term fiscal sustainability. And we will need to put a greater value on grey wisdom and experience.

The end of the change management era

As I have said elsewhere, I've lost count of how many books and articles I have read on change management. I am increasingly of the view that the age of change management is over. Change is management. Gone are the days when you change things every few years or it takes years for a product to get to market.

Increasingly organisations need to evolve their structures and ensure a reasonable proportion of staff are always working just on incubation projects while other staff just concentrate on business-as-usual (BAU). When the incubation is ready to become part of BAU, it needs to be injected into the business with the speed and precision of a mid-air refueling. Forget the laggards and the early adopters. Change needs to be considered as a new organisational imperative, not an exotic animal that you can breed in a box and train people to feed. Without this approach, businesses suffer because their BAU is constantly distracted by an unrelenting change management agenda, complete with bell-curve charts and well-meaning support people with great hair.

Multi-jobs

More than 850,000 Australians work in more than one job. For some this is a way of piecing together an adequate income when they cannot find full-time work or adequate part-time or casual hours in a single job. For others it is a deliberate lifestyle consideration, or a deliberate move based on the lack of a well-paying job in an area of passion. Many literally use a second job to top up their income so they can afford to do something they love. The bulk of multiple-job workers work the equivalent of full-time hours overall. Again, this is not necessarily a bad thing if it gives people variety and economies are unable to generate enough full-time jobs to meet demand.

Work from anywhere

Technology has quickly made the traditional office largely redundant. It is now very common for people to be working with their laptops in coffee shops, at home – anywhere really. While Yahoo's Marissa Mayer famously outlawed work-from-home, it is a reality of many modern workplaces, and has been thoroughly fast-tracked by the COVID-19 pandemic. Presumably, this will continue to impact demand for office space, office design and even the growth of public space areas (libraries, public places etc) designed as informal work areas.

Curiously, this has also created grey areas around sick leave. In the past, if you were sick and contagious you stayed home and watched television. Now, if you are mostly contagious, you can just work at home and keep your germs to yourself. But is that a sick day or not? As discussed in the next chapter, COVID-19 has put this into very sharp focus.

Technology class system

This is an interesting one. The modern working world is divided into three technology classes – fast-moving geeks up for every new app and function on a day-to-day basis; people who are reasonably technically literate but can only identify about 60% of gadgets in the electrical store catalogue; and the technology challenged who pride themselves on not using email or appearing on social media. In this system of technology classes, how do you equip a workplace in a way that keeps everybody functional? Some workplaces need to be current and can only employ the geek class.

Many companies are dealing with the issue by a "bring-your-own-device" policy that allows those frustrated with the pace of the standard-issue work equipment to go into their own hyper-drive zone. Even this trend is now under threat from the need for extraordinary levels of cybersecurity to protect data. Clearly there are challenges knowing when to jump in on technology upgrades when new versions seem to become available on a weekly basis. Most humans are simply not built to evolve their behaviours and practices at Bill Gates' "speed of thought".

2. The COVID-19 blip

Given the moment in history, it is impossible to ignore the COVID-19 global pandemic and its implications for the economy, jobs and the way we live.

Many books will be written on that subject alone. I call it a blip because the jury is still out on whether it is a short-term shock or long-term fundamental history changer, particularly in the context of work.

I suspect future history will judge that the pandemic fast-forwarded a series of changes that were already forming in the minds of workers and companies.

In Brisbane, Australia, where I live, we were lucky to avoid the worst of COVID and experience only very short-term restrictions on our movements and activities. After a few months of relative normality, life sprang back to a close approximation of the pre-COVID world.

Certainly, most people kept hand sanitising and there was some semblance of social distancing, but mostly things went back to a slightly more cautious normal.

Having said that, there are already signs of deeper, accelerated change fast-tracked by the pandemic shock.

The most interesting is working from home (or more aptly "working from anywhere") and the use of digital technology for commerce and communication.

For many years, there have been predictions that huge numbers of people will adopt "telecommuting" and work at home instead of the office. The logical implications of this include a lesser need for rigid office space and less peak hour traffic. It also means new challenges around life balance at home and the requirement for different corporate mindsets around geographical location of workers and work supervision.

Of course, working from home is still only available to a percentage of the workforce. There will always be roles that simply must be performed face to face.

I think there is little doubt that COVID-19 has sped up the work from home experiment. It has shown many companies that these arrangements can work successfully, and video can be a viable (if not ideal) alternative to face-to-face meetings that often burn productivity through excessive travel time.

For every one of these change experiments, there are upsides and downsides.

Working from home, particularly when children are at home, can be highly stressful and create a maelstrom of work and home demands that manifest into a feeling of having no downtime. There are obvious advantages in avoiding commutes and having to just walk to another room to your office. However, it can give you a sense of social isolation and a disconnect from colleagues and the main action.

It could be argued that this isolation can be overcome by improved video call technology. I thought that for a while too, until I experienced the negative health impacts of switching to video.

Plenty of evidence is emerging now to suggest that long days on video are extra exhausting, bad for your eyes and a risk to your posture if you do not maintain a high level of diligence. It is simply not viable to substitute all of your previous face-to-face encounters with video.

I will deal with the issue of workspaces later in this section. In summary, workspace needs were already changing before the pandemic so, like all the other things, it has accelerated change rather than fundamentally changed the path.

In the real world, these are the things I think COVID-19 will change in the medium to long term –

- More workers moving to non-traditional careers and work hours as part of a more integrated work, home and social life
- A growth in genuine workplace flexibility that can be exercised without guilt or taint
- A greater emphasis on health in the workplace in general, and improved systems to deal quickly and efficiently with health threats
- A greater emphasis on employee mental health, particularly when people are working at home by themselves for long periods
- A far lower tolerance for any employee coming to work sick and infecting the rest of the office or factory (This will be coupled with ongoing enhanced hygiene in all work environments. I suspect hand sanitiser in shared spaces is here to stay)
- Employers insisting on being able to verify that home-work stations are safe and not causing long-term health issues
- A lift in the number of people working from outside of the office most of the time
- An increase in people working part of the week at home and a greater propensity for employers to accept that
- A speeding up of office space designs that promote viable dual home and work desks and space that allows location flexibility
- Some reduction in work travel for meetings that are genuinely viable on video

- A greater use of video calls as part of the mix (but moving back to a lower level than we embraced out of necessity during the pandemic)
- A brief respite on commuter congestion in many cities (potentially buying time for some fundamental rethinks around how we want people to move around our cities in the future. This might speed up the evolution to driver-less cars and car-free inner cities)
- Employer-provided home-work stations becoming part of incentive perks in some industries.

It will take a few years to be able to look back properly at this period of history and fully assess the impacts. Hopefully we will ultimately conclude that the pandemic was a wake-up call that prompted us to do a lot of things better and make positive change more quickly.

3. The rise of "stretch" jobs

There was a time when you studied or trained for a job and did that job for most of your life. Your job was easy to explain, and the skills needed were well established.

That was then.

In an economy evolving at the speed of thought, formal qualifications are struggling to keep pace with real needs. Increasingly we are seeing "stretch jobs". Stretch jobs happen in two ways:

Stretching into skills

In an era of rising skills shortages, many employers now are looking to employ smart, agile employees capable of rapid learning (and re-learning) on the job, rather than expecting to find a ready pool of perfectly job-ready candidates.

Most of our traditional training systems simply are not geared for the current state of change.

This has big implications for recruitment. It will increasingly mean finding people who are capable of stretching into a role, and stretching with it, rather than people who have done an identical role before.

This will be a big challenge for the robots who run programs all over the Internet looking for skill and experience matches. They will need to understand what people can do, not just what they have done.

Stretching into multitasks

Small businesses don't have the luxury of large departments and specialisations. These business owners have long been "jacks of all trades" out of necessity.

This will be increasingly important in a constantly disrupting business environment.

Lots of small and medium companies are being highly innovative in building skills within their existing workforces. They are also well versed in finding industry all-rounders who thrive taking on often vastly different types of responsibilities within a single job.

Many are also finding their existing trade workforces can intuitively adapt to environments enhanced by digital technology and robotics.

The workforce of the future will need to be highly adaptive, innovative, and capable of fast evolution and thinking outside the square. Finding and recruiting these people could be a very different art form.

It is becoming increasingly clear that we are entering a workforce paradigm shift. The computer age brought astonishing change to the nature of work but that will be nothing compared to the next wave of digital and artificial intelligence disruption.

This is going to require some big thinking to ensure public policy, skills evolution and economic structural adjustment keep pace with where technology is taking us.

4. Rising trends in the new job market

The future of work is a much-discussed topic, and I do not intend to dwell on it too much in this book, other than to make some observations on the following trends that I expect will emerge from the Worknado over the next 10 years.

Constant adaptation and learning

From a very early age, humans are going to have to be constant and agile learners. It will be less about tangible skills and qualifications for the future and more about "learning to learn" so discovery and new skills are just part of how we live and the way we think.

70-year careers

Some researchers are even suggesting 100-year careers. That will probably come well into the future. But, certainly, children currently starting school can reasonably expect to be in the workforce into their 80s and 90s as attitudes towards aging change and there is a further shift towards humans mostly doing knowledge and service work.

This is a good thing. With most menial and heavy physical work disappearing behind us, the traditional idea of retirement is obsolete. There is something bizarre about ordinary workers still thinking about retirement in their 60s while US presidential candidates are mostly just getting warmed up at that age and US President Joe Biden was elected at 78.

Claiming back free time

Various economic seismic jolts, particularly the 2008-09 Global Financial Crisis, have created a rebooted culture of long hours and "face time" in many workplaces. It feels like we are on the cusp of major social correction where this simply will not be tolerated.

As per my last point, people will need to work until they are much older in the new-world economy. They cannot do this if they do not work sustainably. Overworked people wear out. Our societies also can't handle the rising tide of mainstream mental illness from overstretched lives. In a more technologically advanced time, humans should finally demand back the life balance that science and innovation have been promising us for decades.

Freelancing, brokers and work campuses

It is clear from the number of redundancies in contemporary workforces that the organisational structures of the past 50 years are not adapting well to an environment of more rapid change. It is easy to imagine a future where most people have a collection of skills that move around effectively on a freelance basis. We will most likely all have brokers or "agents" who are searching for our next project for us while we complete the current project. You could argue many recruitment firms have already morphed in this direction.

Physical workplaces will change off the back of that. There will be far more "campus" workplaces where people come together for specific projects rather than the old-style big corporate offices.

Working from anywhere

This is already happening, but more and more firms (particularly office-style workplaces) will just let people work from wherever they want. Staff will only come together in the office for designated contact time to retain cohesion and connection for strategic direction and socialisation. As previously outlined, the COVID-19 pandemic had fast-tracked this trend.

Automation and artificial intelligence

I will not dwell on this because so much has been written on the subject, except to say that this is an incredible opportunity to advance the human experience. Yes, automation takes jobs. But, as a civilisation, we have shown remarkable resilience to this type of change.

Letting machines do what they can do better than humans should free us to advance the arts, creativity, new social endeavours and a rebirth of community and connectivity. New jobs and types of working will emerge from that.

Greater autonomy

There are many interesting examples around the world of organisations that have abandoned traditional hierarchy structures in favour of self-managing teams. These models probably fail more often than they succeed (although some have done spectacularly well) but they are further examples of a growing desire by humans to have greater control of their lives and environments. We are seeing the same thing with many young people opting for start-ups rather than the traditional corporate machines. This is a trend that is likely to continue in the new world.

Unexpected service workers

One of the big challenges, even in the current workforce, is the loss of jobs previously held predominantly by male blue-collar workers. We don't seem to have a plan for these people.

On paper, in the new wave economy this group will probably need to either be trained for higher skilled work where possible or be reinvented in the service industries. We need far more policy work on this. It is a question of deconstructing the skills of the old world and reconstructing them in a different form. I doubt this will happen without some clever thinking. But it must be done if we are to avoid an underclass of domestic economic refugees.

5. Innovation and incubation

The word innovation is one of the most overused in the English language. Even though it has been in the language for a very long time, sometimes it is treated like something we only discovered in the past 10 years.

Innovation is no longer just a long word that describes doing things better. It has become a whole industry complete with sticky notes, white boards, brainstorming sessions, deep dives, online sharing gizmos and shark tanks.

Companies are constantly told they need to innovate. Governments unrelentingly write cheques to facilitate this, boards ask their CEOs what they are doing about it and the bookstores are awash with publications explaining how to do it.

In many different organisations, I've seen many different approaches to the innovation imperative:

- Innovation "systems" through which staff submit ideas so they can be assessed
- Massive innovation "programs" in which staff spend hours attending workshops and populating sticky notes so innovation is seen to be democratised and inclusive
- Committees of bright thinkers who drive or collect ideas and create business plans
- Leadership programs with "projects" designed to give companies ready-made, ready-to-implement initiatives to improve efficiency or profitability
- Deep dives designed to produce great ideas and products in a few days
- Shark tanks where people with ideas stand nervously in front of people who control money seeking investment in their ideas
- Suggestion boxes that allow ideas to be submitted anonymously to management
- Staff prizes for people who come up with the best ideas.

In my experience, most of these innovation approaches have some value and are better than having no pro-active way to give oxygen to fresh ideas.

Having said that, many also give a poor return on investment and often become so bureaucratic that they can be idea killers rather than nurturing genuine, positive change. All the innovation "systems" I have seen in operation ended up spending many man hours assessing staff ideas and rejecting nearly all of them.

The ones that simply fed ideas to the existing management also tended to mostly fail because managers are busy and, unless the idea is so good that it demands immediate and urgent attention, the new idea did not make their short list. Staff often talk about ideas "dying on the vine".

The other problem is that few companies genuinely invest money in developing new ideas unless they have been proven elsewhere, there is a burning platform of need or business is going so well that there is cash to burn for trialing some stuff.

Often the projects that come out of leadership courses are very good but, in the companies I have worked for who did these programs, my best guess is that about one in 50 projects ever saw the light of day in the real world.

In fact, these leadership course projects tend to be more valuable when they are used to value-add something a company is already committed to doing, rather than promoting genuine, clean-piece-of-paper innovative thinking.

Sticky notes as a basis for innovation are hopefully a passing fad. It is quick and looks inclusive but seldom does much thought go into them and often the wrong people are in the room (hierarchy-based rather than based on the generation of fresh thinking).

I have seen the staff prizes for good ideas work quite well, provided the prizes are for things actually implemented rather than ideas that might have some value in the future.

There are some clear obstacles to innovation in most companies:

- Busy people are expected to do it as part of their day job. As a result, it is seldom a priority.
- Companies typically claim to have three-to-five-year plans but mostly they have one-year plans and that is not enough time to plan and implement real innovation.
- New programs are often driven by outside consultants but very typically not enough is subsequently invested in the implementation and immersion. As a result, new things are built outside the company but get rejected by the culture when attempts are made to implement them. It is a bit like creating a new organ for a body in a laboratory and then inserting it into the body. There is every chance that the body will reject it.

Having watched so many of these programs at close quarters, I am not sure any of them are ideal and some have wasted a scary amount of money to produce little result.

For me, innovation does not work when it is a systemised "program". It only works when it is a corporate mindset, and the organisation seeks out people with an unrelenting dissatisfaction with the status quo.

I have sat in senior executive meetings in which everyone spends a lot of time talking about how we can be more innovative. Bizarrely these were already some of the most innovative people I had worked with. They all woke up every day thinking about how they could do things better. And they were all in a position to implement positive change.

There is a real danger in believing that you need to create a corporate structure around mindsets. You don't. You just need to create the ecosystem where ideas thrive and give leaders permission to try things, even things that might not always work.

The other vital ingredient for genuine innovation is an incubation capacity. Given the speed of change required to keep pace with contemporary business needs, it is a fallacy to believe that people can just implement change as part of their day jobs. While I am opposed to highly programmed innovation, I am a big believer in creating incubation capacity.

Any sizable business needs people working on the incubation of new things all the time. Incubation is a different thing to innovation. Innovation is about driving an ideas culture. Incubation is about having a structure to scope, design, test, implement and review new ideas.

Incubation is a special skill. And it cannot be done in isolation from people who run the relevant areas of the business.

This is partly because we no longer have the luxury to do change management as a stop and restart exercise. Innovation and change must be constant. We need to have the ability to refuel companies mid-air and this can only happen when incubation teams are working in parallel with business-as-usual and there is a constant improvement mentality.

Again, the incubation needs to be owned by the organisation and its people – not outsiders – and we should always ask our own people first on the best way forward.

People in the organisation need to believe that innovation is doable, and incubation is properly resourced. Otherwise you run the risk of wearing out your best people and eventually burning out your company. There is a fine line between a company being crippled by change and energised by it.

Overlayed with this is the need to adopt a version of McKinsey's three horizons approach to long-term competitiveness. This requires a constant program of businesses as usual and forward planning:

Horizon 1 – Things that we do now

Horizon 2 – Things that are implemented or about to be implemented but have not reached a stabilisation point yet

Horizon 3 – Projects to drive new areas of profitable business in the future

It is also vital for companies to have a genuine 5-year strategy plan and have things earmarked for each year, not all jammed into the first 18 months.

Couple that with an innovation mindset, employing people who drive ideas and know how to implement them, and innovation is not all that hard. And it does not require too many sticky notes!

6. Fractured pathways

In simpler times, people obtained a trade or a degree, applied for a job with a solid company, worked for 40 years and got a nice send-off with a gold watch, an earnest speech and a home-made sponge cake.

For others, their dads or their uncles "got them on" at the plant; they sat an aptitude exam for government or big business after they finished school, or they just scanned the positions vacant ads and applied for something that would pay the bills.

Today, not only are the job pathways more complex; the transitions have become fractured and, in some cases, dysfunctional. This seemed to become particularly pronounced after the Global Financial Crisis more than a decade ago as we adapted to an economy that dragged itself up with a hangover rather than bounding out of bed.

The following are some of my observations on the buckles that have appeared in the employment train tracks.

School to university

Having watched a few groups go through this now, I fear something serious is missing in this transition. The first year after school has always been a tough one with 12 years of uniforms and structures suddenly replaced by a more free-wheeling existence.

Today the contrast is even greater. High school has become so fully scheduled, coached, controlled and results-obsessed that the first year out is like going from the army to a hippy commune. What's more, there is still pressure for 17-year-olds during high stress final year exam periods to decide what they want to study at university and, by extension, have some sense of what they want to do with their lives. Most don't really have a clue.

Equally, during school you tend to have lots of friends because you are all required by law to turn up every day and hang out together. It is state-sanctioned socialisation. Without that discipline, it is so easy just to lose social connections because friendship becomes a more proactive endeavour. I'm sure many teenagers are quietly struggling with this.

It feels like we are missing some sort of transition year: a more generalist introduction to tertiary study or workforce preparation that teaches disciplines vital for all areas of working life. This could include strategy, effective communication, workforce dynamics, a basic sense of the law and how it works and the basic tenets of business and government.

I wonder if a year of this type of approach might be a better way to bridge the after-school gap, not unlike what was done with middle school/junior high to bridge that other difficult transition between primary and high school. At the very least students need better support in that first post-school year. An extraordinary number seem to struggle. I think this is something we should be discussing more often.

Wasted or misdirected study

It is well documented that countless millions of dollars are being "wasted" on education and training that is never used in any practical way.

When you add up the people who finish degrees but don't use them, those who change mid-way and those who start study and then drop out, it is hard to escape a conclusion of chronic waste. Some would argue that no study is wasted in a holistic context, but higher education is a big public investment and there must be better ways to create pathways and transitions that more appropriately match people with outcomes.

We are already seeing the rise of more pragmatic approaches to higher education. These include:

- The rise of bespoke and creatively packaged courses and degrees
- Micro-credentials that can be undertaken quickly
- Official credentialing of skills obtained on-the-job

University to work

This is a not a new problem, but it seems to have become harder in recent years. I suspect that after the shock of the Global Financial Crisis more than a decade ago, many companies started running lean and were too spooked to commit heavily to in-house training. As a result, fewer of them were prepared to hire a graduate at full pay and invest the time to train them. They also feared that if they invested in training someone, they would lose them to another employer anyway.

The result is a lot of graduates working for free as interns. Again, there is nothing inherently wrong with this, provided it is for a set time based on a real program to teach genuine skills and help them become more employable. Still, I have read many sobering posts from young people lamenting a litany of free gig after free gig with nothing at the end of it, and still bills to pay.

This is another area where it feels like it is time for a new pathway. The workforce has a tradition of apprenticeships, cadetships and traineeships, but the transition from graduate to work remains rocky and ad hoc.

With employers reluctant to pay graduates full wages and graduates sometimes working for nothing as interns, is it time for a better debate on a compromise system that makes it easier for both? At the moment it just feels like lose-lose.

Fast-change employment

In a previous job I was conducting a one-on-one meeting with a newly hired employee and I asked her if she saw the role as something she would do long-term. "Absolutely," she replied, "if it works out, I will probably stay for a whole year".

Employers still tend to see an employee leaving after one or two years as some sort of failure. Yet you do not have to look too hard on LinkedIn profiles to realise that this is now very common, particularly among ambitious younger workers.

As with most locked-in change, it is far better to find ways to flow with a trend than to fight it. The hyper-churn is probably more a reflection of the speed of change and business reinvention than any fundamental failure on the part of an employer.

I suspect many workplaces need to have a two-speed workforce – a solid, rusted-on core and a frequently-mobile, fast-changing team that deliver projects and programs and then move on. Churn can just mean you are attracting the best people on the way up, and they have a limited attention span.

50s to retirement

There is a great line in the Jewel Kilcher song *Fading* that asks: "What happens to us, when we get old and in the way? I guess she answered me 'cause they took me away."

The zone from 50s to retirement has become a perplexing one for many people. And sometimes it does seem like individuals just disappear from the workforce in many industries once they reach this zone.

For a start, retirement is no longer a finishing line. It is more like a blurry mirage that appears off in the distance but never really materialises in any solid form.

For some older workers the battle is to retain a value reputation as hungry, younger staff move up the ranks. Experience and wisdom should be in high demand. Yet often this can be seen as being caught up in the past or "past your prime".

For others it is just the challenge of working out what to do. Many people are peaking early in their jobs, taking on senior management in their 30s and 40s. But what does that leave for the 50s and 60s? There are only so many CEO and managing director roles. I think this is why so many of this group start businesses or consultancies or do some form of dropping out or dropping down.

It sometimes feels like the workforce just hasn't really worked out what to do with 50 and 60-somethings. This is a shame. They should be our prime employment herd.

7. The end of agism?

As a young reporter one of my first assignments was to interview a retiring coal miner who had worked in the earth's dark underbelly for more than 40 years.

At the age of 18, the idea of 40 years seemed like an eternity and I asked how he had endured for so long.

"It really doesn't feel like 40 years," he confessed. "In fact, it only seems like yesterday that I was your age. And inside my head I really don't feel any different than I did then."

For some reason those words have always stuck with me and, as I get older, the truism of life's unrelenting time march becomes even more pronounced.

But, in the 30-odd years since that interview, things have changed. Back then, an Australian male could expect to live about five years after a standard retirement. Today, based on the same retirement age, a large proportion of the population are on track to be retired for as many years as they worked.

Around the world governments are pushing back the official retirement age. The very thought messes with our sense of entitlement in countries where paying taxes and working hard are synonymous with earning the right to comfortable, largely government-funded twilight years.

However, as the following points reveal, this is a debate that we will need to bring on.

Old age is a relatively new phenomenon

Researcher and author Fred Pearce (*Peoplequake*) says it is quite possible that half of all the human beings who have ever lived past the age of 65 are alive today. The rules of demography and longevity have changed, and only recently. We still have much to do to factor aging properly into our societal structures and mindsets.

Working longer and living to really advanced years often go hand in hand

In 1958, polling agency Gallup discovered that, for men who lived to the age of 95 and beyond, the average retirement age was 80. But these men were not just working for the sake of it. Whether they were collecting supermarket trollies for a living or doing office filing, they liked what they did and found it engaging and meaningful.

Sometimes old age is a mindset imposed by social norms

In his brilliant book, *Before Happiness,* Shawn Achor cites a 1979 study by Harvard psychologist Ellen Langer in which she was able to reverse the effects of ageing on a group of 75-year-old men by having them pretend they were 20 years younger.

Basically, Langer took her subjects from a nursing home environment with cafeteria meals, scheduled recreation and a community of mostly elderly strangers and took them back to the world of 1959.

She did this by using a converted monastery to recreate the clothes, music, television, books and magazines of the era. Instead of reminiscing about the past, they were living it again. And nobody treated them as old people. By the end of the experiment, the majority of the group had improved physical strength, posture, memory, and cognitive function. The experiment largely backed the notion that you are only as old as you act.

Living past 100 is becoming much more common

It is now clear that growing numbers of people will live past 100, something unthinkable a century ago. This will fundamentally change the type of lives we live. According to *The 100-Year Life* by Lynda Gratton and Andrew Scott a child born in the West today has a greater than 50 percent chance of living past 105. The same book relates that Japan used to give a silver sake dish to everyone who turned 100 in that country. In 1963 it was given to 153 people. By 2014 the number had grown to 29,350, and it was discontinued a year later. Similarly, the British monarch has long written to anyone who turns 100 in the Commonwealth. Over a single decade, the number of people administering these cards rose from one to seven.

Many people do not transition well to retirement

In 2012 the Harvard School of Public Health studied 5422 ageing individuals and found those who had retired were 40% more likely to have had a heart attack or stroke than those who were still working. This mostly happened soon after retirement. A sudden shift from work to retirement can be very unhealthy.

Large numbers are already working longer

All over the Western world we are seeing rising numbers of people working well past the previous "official" retirement age. Many countries have lifted the qualification age for pension and insurance schemes to reflect the longer life spans and resulting longer years in the workforce. There is also evidence that increasing numbers of older people are reactivating their economic lives after retirement through online work and businesses and taking part in the so-called "gig economy".

Stressful jobs and long life sometimes happen together

There is a common myth that stressful jobs lead to early deaths. This is not necessarily so. American presidents are a good case in point.

A 2011 study by Chicago demographer S. Jay Olshansky found presidents generally lived longer than expected for men of the same age and era. In fact, 23 of the 34 US presidents who died from natural causes lived longer than statistically expected. The average lifespan of the first eight presidents was 79.8 years at a time when the life expectancy for the average man was 40! Modern presidents have also enjoyed long lives. Ronald Reagan and Gerald Ford both lived to 93. George HW Bush lived to 94.

The election of Joe Biden to the Presidency at 78 will help

to reset perceptions around age. There is something inherently inconsistent between the willingness to elect someone of that age to one of the most demanding jobs in the world, and the expectation that workers will move out of paid work in their sixties.

What does this mean?

The long life of many world leaders highlights one of the key lessons about aging and retirement. Clearly wealth, privilege and access to top medical care can extend your life no matter how stressful some of your jobs are.

It is also clear that there are jobs, and jobs. Mentally stimulating jobs performed in a climate of general good health, proper eating, genetic luck, physical activity and supportive friends and family don't seem to have a use-by date.

But who would begrudge the man I interviewed 30-odd years ago having a comfortable retirement at 65 after so many years of physical work in dark and dusty coal mines?

The retirement debate should not be about picking a magical age at which all humans become unable or disinclined to be in the workforce.

It should be about developing a flexible system that gives people whole-of-life options – working, winding down, winding back up and retirement choices. We need to end the traditional hard-wired notion of a national retirement age. It results in a chronic waste of skills, experience, and opportunity, and sits awkwardly with the human condition and aspiration in the third millennium. I recently attended an Elton John concert and it was clear that everybody in the band was well into age groups traditionally associated with retirement. Thankfully nobody told them that. The youthful energy was incredible.

8. Video killed the meeting room star

In the 1960s and 1970s all the futuristic television shows and movies had cool versions of "video phones". They were an accepted part of our sci-fi-esque future state, along with matching tracksuits, flying cars and the ability to "beam up" rather than walk or drive.

The Jetsons had them. *2001 – A Space Odyssey* had them. Every B-grade black-and-white space movie had them. *Star Trek's* Captain Kirk had the coolest video phone – large, full colour, high-definition screen with surround sound, and the ability to face-time random passing aliens at will.

I remember thinking as a child that it would be so cool in the future if we actually had video phones.

And then we got them...

When the "video phone" entered our lives, it was not the social revolution we had been expecting. In fact, it was more of a passé ripple. It kind-of just happened. Overnight we had video capability on mobile phones, on computers and in meeting rooms with giant screens almost as good as Captain Kirk's.

On almost any call or meeting we could beam in like a random passing alien and look people in the eye wherever they were around the world.

But mostly we didn't…

By then we were already in social retreat. Phone calls had given way to emails and texting. Research showed humans had far fewer friends than in the past and much of our socialisation had been swallowed by a new time-poor reality.

The Internet allowed us to hide in public and live our lives as a social media timeline, illustrated with carefully chosen pictures and witty observations about trivial things.

By then we had also moved away from the random drop-in. When I was a child growing up in a country town, socialising consisted mostly of drop-ins. To the back door, not the front! You didn't make appointments, you just dropped in. People expected it. They always had cake, just in case.

Today the drop-in is almost gone. In fact, I find I even make appointments to phone people now. Lives are not random. They are organised in half-hour blocks controlled by Outlook. Mess with the schedule and you talk to the hand, or the voicemail.

Then came the pandemic…

In just a few weeks there was a big change. When we were first forced into a corporate life dominated by unrelenting video chats and conference calls, meetings were mostly attended by giant initials surround by circles. Occasionally the initials were replaced with studio shots of people taken 10 years ago.

Then, bit by bit, the mouse snuck over to the camera button and actual people started to appear. And not just the usual corporate people in suits, smart dresses and salon-quality hair. The corporate video world was full of people with home haircuts, work-in-progress grooming and self-styled dress codes framed with arbitrary acts of ordinary human life in the background.

It seemed like overnight corporate humans had emerged from behind a facade to reveal their true selves. *The Wizard of Oz* was out from the curtain to reveal he is just a regular man.

After a while even the fake Italian scenes and blurred backgrounds that sometimes cut off your ears started to switch off. The year 2020 became the historical marker when we finally felt comfortable sharing the real backdrops of our lives.

Here we were again. Humans acting like humans. Sometimes we even used this curious *Star Trek* technology to just drop in on someone. And it was okay. We didn't even need to tell Outlook.

So, what does all this mean?

It might mean nothing. This whole period might just be a passing, slightly dreamlike, blip on the radar of our lives before we go about our business like there is nothing to see here.

Or maybe it is the time when the old world of socialising and the new world of real time digital connection merged into a new era of human eye-to-eye interaction.

People keep saying we are all in this together. The fact is that, as a human race, we have always been in everything together. Now is the time to finally realise that, no matter where our desks sit in the world, our backgrounds look uncannily similar.

9. The gender tragedy

For a while I really believed we were getting there. Women seemed to be dominating education, snaring lots of senior jobs and emerging everywhere as CEOs and directors. The old stereotypes were breaking down; women had momentum and confidence. Equality – tick. Everyone take a bow. High fives all-around.

Now I am not so sure. I am not sure at all.

I fear that after the Global Financial Crisis and the temporary reprieve from the skills shortage, workplaces went hyper-pragmatic and seemed to be in a state of constant dread. Continuous corporate disruption has left what seems like a pseudo-permanent pall over the corporate landscape and changed the psyche.

There are two clear side effects:

1. We were back to the situation we had in the mid-1990s in which everyone felt the need to be seen to be working crazy hours for job security.

2. It exposed the fact that, despite decades of progress, women are still taking most of the responsibility for childcare and household management (as well as holding down jobs). In this new knuckle-down economic and corporate paradigm, women are generally the biggest losers. Men work harder and longer in their day jobs, and many drop the ball at home. Many women just try to do everything and live with a constant "which thing will I half-do today" feeling.

The result is that much of the progress to make women's, and to a lesser extent, men's lives more balanced and achievable has gone backwards.

These are some of the signs that things are askew:

Women with kids spend a lot of time apologising

Have you noticed this? Hard-working, highly skilled women have to pick their kids up from some form of childcare. They have to go. They have put in their hours. Yet, they feel guilty about it because so many other people are still in the office. When did we get it so wrong that something as important as making sure kids are safely collected becomes a source of guilt? There is something seriously erroneous with that picture. The needs of young children have to be a collective community responsibility. Remember the adage that it takes a village to raise a child.

It still does, and workplaces are an important part of the village.

We treat part-time work as a problem

Many women (and some men) with young children cannot work five days. It just does not work. They need shorter weeks or their kids and home life suffer. So, what do we do? Typically, the part-time request becomes a problem: "We really need someone fulltime, someone who is really committed to the role". Or even worse, we take highly experienced women and automatically treat a part-time job as a lesser job – lower hourly rate, lesser responsibilities, disconnected from the strategic core. The attitude towards job sharing is generally similar.

Often accommodating part-time work and job sharing is hard. That is no reason not to do it. Most things worth doing are hard. And what if we treated it as an opportunity to be more creative with our organisational structures rather than as an inconvenient asterisk on the organisational chart? We could retain talent, foster loyalty and keep families functional. Corporate social responsibility begins here.

Nobody celebrates working smarter

Despite the plethora of evidence that long hours (often just for show) are not good for anybody, including corporations, we still have a habit of celebrating and rewarding this type of behaviour. It would be far more logical to celebrate smart working – the ability to achieve just as much in a shorter timeframe and lead a balanced life. It is as if we just can't bring ourselves to do it. It is worth remembering the famous children's story in which only the child was brave enough to admit the emperor had no clothes. Sometimes we are all too complicit in the dumb acceptance of things we know to be ludicrous.

The transition back to work after childbirth is generally hard

No matter how far we come with equality, and no matter how many men take on primary child carer roles, women are going to be the ones having babies and this will put them at a career disadvantage. This is a simple case where we need to over-correct for one gender to ensure that pregnancy is a light speed bump on the career highway, not a detour onto a gravel road that may never lead back to the main road. I can't speak for women, but my observation is that, in most workplaces, getting back into work mode after pregnancy is particularly difficult. Yet I'm not aware of many organisations that have specific support programs for this. It is more like – welcome back, there's your desk, there's your phone, here's your work – good luck with that.

Our span of hours still reflects a 1950s mentality

The growth of the knowledge economy and the rapid advent of portable technology means we are in the best shape ever to allow genuine work flexibility. But mostly we don't. Our span of hours for work still largely reflects a 1950s mentality and a notion that work is somewhere we go rather than something we do. For many people with family responsibilities, it might make sense to work a few hours in the morning and then resume from 9pm until midnight, for example. In a large number of jobs, such an approach would have no detrimental impact on work outcomes. In fact, it might give us access to more highly skilled female workers for longer periods.

And imagine if lots of people worked at home for a couple of hours in the morning so they could use their brain's most productive time for creative work rather than mind-numbing commuting. This might also mean we could spend less on road infrastructure that mostly serves just two peak-hour times a day. And it would be easier to get a seat on the train or the bus.

Where next?

It seems obvious from all the research that long hours do not make us more productive. In fact, nearly all the credible research points to crazy hours and long stretches sitting at a desk making us unhappier, unhealthier, less creative, and less efficient.

The way we have evolved has often created workplaces that are often anti-family, anti-health, anti-productivity and completely illogical.

We need to get real here. Weekdays are becoming void of any real social, community or family time, many women are being asked to juggle competing priorities that are close to impossible, vital sleeping hours are falling and, around the world, the unrelenting nature of modern life is sending cases of stress and anxiety off the charts (check the figures – it's scary). We are overdue for a seismic social correction.

We cannot leave the change agenda only to a few strong women with the guts to speak up about how hard it is for them to juggle all the demands on them. Men need to champion this too - loudly, and confidently.

This is not a problem we need governments or legislation to solve. It is purely about the attitudes of management and the psyche of our organisations. This is one we can fix tomorrow.

Thankfully, the COVID-19 pandemic seems to have finally opened a real conversation on this topic. And the forced socio-corporate experiment has largely verified the value of genuine workplace flexibility.

It is not without challenges, but many more employers are far more open to building work around humans rather than stretching humans around work. Hopefully this era will eventually be marked as the start of a genuine gender-neutral workplace.

10. Why are we so afraid of part-time work?

As outlined in the previous chapter, in an era when we give so much lip service to work-life balance and equal opportunity, the attitude of many organisations towards part-time work seems oddly out of whack with contemporary needs.

Lots of people, male and female, simply cannot meet all of their life commitments and hold down a traditional 38-hour, five-day work week. If they try, they live with constant time stress and a feeling that home and work are both suffering, and their lives are stuck on an out-of-control carousel. This is not good for anyone, or for societal health in general.

These jobs barely exist

If you look at any major job site, the number of "real" jobs advertised as part-time (as distinct from casual) are tiny (generally between 2% and 4%) and few employers offer up jobs that can be either full-time or part-time.

Most of the professional people I know who work part-time have had to really work their professional networks or compromise their seniority to snare a part-time role. Many lament that asking for part-time work is perceived as a weakness; like they have to apologise for trying to balance their lives.

This is yet another symptom of our growing inability to celebrate smart, lifestyle-friendly work over the rigidity of a post-industrial revolution structure that is as dated as 1970s cop shows and mullet hair.

Negotiating down

Typically, in the corporate world the only way to get a decent, permanent part-time job is to start with five days and negotiate down after a period. Alternatively, people can apply for a full-time role and try to negotiate down as part of the recruitment process.

Neither option is easy. I know of a recent case where someone applied for a position advertised as full-time and asked for part-time during the interview only to find out later that the request was considered an outrage. You'd swear the person had tried to defraud them out of their silverware.

"How dare you have the audacity to ask for part-time!" was the attitude, and this from an organisation that markets itself as contemporary and cutting edge. Sometimes I wonder if we are really in the 21st century or we went through some worm hole back to the 1950s.

Things I have seen work

Despite the structural obstacles, I've been lucky enough to work in a few organisations that make a genuine effort to support part-time work. And I've never personally had a problem with supporting it to keep and attract talented people in a way that allows them to live a sane life.

I've seen the following work plenty of times:

Job sharing

There are plenty of examples of successful sharing of a single full-time job between two people. If they are committed, you get great results, and the benefit of two brains. My daughter had job sharing teachers in primary school. It worked beautifully.

The overlapper

Sometimes jobs can be budgeted at 1.2 headcount (two times a three-day headcount) and overlap a day for continuity.

Fitting five into four

Many people I know who work four-day weeks seem to do as much work in four days as many others do in five. They learn to be smart and pragmatic with their weeks.

School-hours jobs

Most of our deadlines are self-imposed. There are seldom really good reasons people can't work school hours, or take a long, late lunchbreak to see their children safely home from school.

Split day/night jobs

It doesn't work for everyone or every role, but I have worked with people who successfully did a few hours during their day and finished their shift from home later in the night.

Part-time work is not always possible (and there are roles where it is simply not practical for a variety of reasons). But this should be the exception rather than the rule. Until we adapt work to the real needs of families, we will continue to be a lesser society and let old-world thinking hold back our human potential.

11. Workspaces

For a long time, office workspaces were fairly standardised. When you started a job, you were shown your desk. It usually had a computer, a coffee cup from an obsolete marketing campaign, some draws, a small bookcase, and stationery from two decades ago that had been passed down by all the people who used that particular desk. If you were lucky you got an ergonomic chair that you could adjust to suit your actual human dimensions.

On your first day you placed a picture of your family and your dog on the desk and replaced your office-issue coffee cup with your own. If you were male and had children, the coffee cup usually said: "World's Greatest Dad".

If you were in a reasonably senior job, your desk came with walls and was called an "office". If you had a corner office with a window you were special, and everybody hated you.

This most basic of standardised workspace has served us well and will probably dominate our office landscapes for some time to come.

However, like many things in the Worknado, the forces of change are swirling around our office desks.

For the past decade or so, much has been written about the growth of "campus" offices. These are shared office environments where, instead of having your own territory with your cup on it to claim it as your own, you just work in whatever space is available. This could be within the corporate office environment or provided by a third party that specialises in providing this sort of space.

Shared first-come-first-served desks are known as "hot desks". The name apparently evolved from the concept of "hot racking" where sailors who worked different shifts were able to use the same bunk at different times.

Hot desking has been around since at least the 1990s but the evolution has been patchy at best. In my experience, hot desks in the corporate environment are mostly used by people visiting from other offices or people who nearly always work at home. They also seem to be considered expendable when there is a need to find a permanent desk for someone who comes to the office every day.

The other big trend of the past 10 years has been an acceleration of "open plan" offices. This effectively means getting rid of the walls and the offices and putting everyone out "on the floor".

This has two potential advantages. Firstly, it breaks down the communication walls as well as the physical walls, encouraging employees at all levels to collaborate in real time through real conversations. The theory goes that this reduces meeting times and keeps the bosses more in touch with what really goes on.

There are also cost advantages. You can fit a lot more people into your office square metreage if you get rid of the walls and create one big cattle pen. This saves on rent and helps to maximise profit and yield from each employee.

Usually, an open plan environment comes with a wall of shared offices, or "quiet rooms" designed for use when you need privacy, a meeting or to have a loud conversation that might disturb colleagues.

The open plan can have some significant downsides for managers. The couple of times I have done it (voluntarily), I have found that I misjudged how many confidential conversations I had in a day. I either ended up almost permanently camped in a shared office or meeting room, or I had to keep going outside or into a stairwell to take confidential calls.

It also took me a long time to block out all the noise from calls and conversations around me. I'm quite social at work but I also need time to get work done. When I work in an office, people tend to come and talk to me when they have a question, or they need to talk something through. In open plan I felt like I was in a conversation most of the day with people around me. If I'm honest, this probably made work more enjoyable. At the same time my productivity probably fell by 30%.

I've been to quite a few businesses using the open plan/spare offices combination and there are mixed views on its success. Many found that the spare offices were never used. At heart people were nesters. They preferred their own desk, even when there were inadequacies.

In a post-pandemic world, with so many people trained to work at home and so many health risks around, the forces of change in this aspect of work world are likely to speed up. The trouble is that each of the forces for change come with a paradox as the logic of space sharing clashes with the risks around sharing contagions.

With respect to hot desks, they make more sense than ever. If more people work more days at home in the future, then companies can save a lot of money by having banks of heavily utilised hot desks rather than paying for lots of individual desks or offices for people who might only use them once or twice a week.

The paradox is that anything shared comes with heightened health risks. This was particularly the case during the pandemic when any common area was a potential risk. However, even in normal circumstances, that is the case. Before COVID-19 we took it for granted that people came to work coughing and sneezing and we lost time each year to illness. In the future there will be less tolerance of that. In most cases, people who are sick will not be allowed to attend work and sanitising is likely to stay with us for a long time.

Similarly, with open plan, the more we herd people into paddocks without distancing or offices, the more we breathe on each other and spread germs.

The other hot desk paradox relates to video. During the pandemic there has been a quantum shift to video meetings. These are no longer just done in the video meeting rooms. Everyone does them at their desk. They can be done at open plan desks, but it is not ideal. There will be pressure to put more noise reduction around every desk. Eventually every desk will look like a mini office.

Employers are also grappling with the dilemma of who is responsible for an employee's home office. Most take the view that they provide equipment for one office space and, if an employee wants a second one at home, it is their responsibility.

There is, however, growing pressure to ensure home work stations are safe and ergonomically sound for employees who work at home over long periods. There will also be questions around office and equipment and responsibility for it if there are less viable workstations available in the office.

It feels to me like the old world of office spaces has entered a new era of transition. The old designs are becoming increasingly obsolete, and, in most offices, we have not really nailed new designs that are ideal.

Overlaying the structural change and pandemic forces, is a growing desire by workers to have variety in their day. Psychologists talk about positivity and job satisfaction being enhanced by having "novel" experiences during our days.

I can relate to that. For most of 2020 and 2021 I spent the bulk of the day sitting at my desk at home working off a video screen. It is boring and draining. We need variety.

I find I work best if I can break up the day with physical meetings and even take my computer to a coffee shop for half an hour to get a different vantage point. I also find a week with some time working uninterrupted at home and some time in the office maximises my productivity.

Much of the change in workspaces in the years ahead will be dictated by highly skilled employees demanding workspaces where they feel healthy, comfortable and productive. There will also be a lot of pressure on employers to create more novel workdays where we feel like humans rather than worker ants.

Watch this space. And these workspaces.

12. Work cultures for the new world

When I was at school, I went to watch my sister in an interschool debate. The topic was that "there is no Australian culture".

I was about 12 at the time. The thing I found most interesting was listening to the teams try to define the word culture. Culture is one of those curious things that doesn't exist in a box; you can't draw it or photograph it. It is a collection of things that leaves behind a residual that is real, but not tangible.

You could well argue that the cultures we live and work in are some of the most important influences on our lives. But where do they come from? Can we influence them? Who really drives them?

The *Oxford Dictionary of Philosophy* has a basic explanation of culture, defined as "the way of life of a people, including their attitudes, values, beliefs, arts, sciences, modes of perception, and habits of thought and activity." That is a fairly useful definition and demonstrates just how many aspects of life feed into this thing we call culture.

The second part of the definition is even more interesting. It suggests that cultural behaviours are learned but "are often too persuasive to be readily noticed from within".

Therein lies the challenge for workplaces. We spend a lot of time in contemporary corporations working on strategy. Yet we all accept the cliché that culture eats strategy for breakfast.

My observation from working in almost 20 different workplaces over the course of my career is that culture is the main driver of an organisation's long-term success. It determines:

- Whether you can attract good people
- Whether people do their best work
- The appetite for new ideas and taking some risks
- The way customers and colleagues are treated
- The way people feel when they go to work in the morning and when they head home at the end of the day
- The levels of palpable stress among staff
- Levels of absenteeism
- Whether people feel valued and cared for.

I have also been astounded at the power of culture to bend human behaviours and lull people into norms that are completely at odds with their personal values and beliefs.

Fighting culture can be exhausting. After a while people start accepting workplace attitudes and the ways things are done without any written protocols or sets of rules. Humans tend to conform to behaviour in these circumstances, even if they are uncomfortable with it. When we are in work cultures that mess with our values, we tend to be steadily dying inside and resenting ourselves.

It can be equally stressful in workplaces that have multiple powerful cultures. This is remarkably common and results in the formation of powerful factions where like-minded people form blocs and use their numbers to manipulate the organisation towards their own world view.

In the worst cases, CEOs and senior leaders find themselves with constantly conflicting advice and a lot of energy and productivity wasted on backroom lobbying rather than healthy, robust front room debates.

For me the healthiest workplaces have a single, all-pervasive culture but multiple different voices that bring diverse perspectives and meaningful advocacy.

To borrow from Shakespeare, the best workplaces are a stage where everyone must play a part. We are all part of one performance but we each have an important role. There are different advocates for people, spending restraint, courageous risks, technology needs, competitive factors and the big picture. Through that, the whole becomes greater than a sum of the parts.

Great leaders intuitively seem to understand the value of these types of teams in building a success culture. They don't surround themselves with "yes people" who just reinforce each other's view or back everything the CEO says. They find people who are on the same page culturally but who trust, respect and value each other enough to have robust discussions that are never personal or insulting. They play the ball, not the man (or woman).

There is more than a subtle difference between multiple voices in an organisation, and multiple factions. Factions tend to fight battles for their views to dominate. Voices contribute to a robust, constructive discussion that leads to the best outcome for the organisation and allows leaders to make good decisions based on a full understanding of the parameters, options and consequences.

Great cultures also tend to have leadership teams that accept and publicly support the final decisions made by the organisation, even when they have a differing view. In toxic cultures, people work to undermine decisions that are contrary to their views, and delight in saying "I told you so" when it does not work out. Great cultures own decisions and outcomes regardless of how they work out.

Really great cultures defend and articulate the views of people who are not in the room, even when the person talking does not agree with the views. This is because they value the collective input and the quality of the final decision ahead of self-interest and winning an argument.

Great workplace cultures have something of an unspoken central idea and mindset that can accommodate a wide range of robust views. There is a set of shared values and goals that everyone buys into. And there is an innate ability for the organisation to find the things that unite it rather than dwelling on the things that divide.

In his autobiography *A Promised Land*, former US President Barack Obama outlines how he was able to unite vastly different demographic groups in Illinois to win a Senate seat. In effect, he collected the shared aspirations of diverse people and became the voice for those.

"Most people, wherever they are from, whatever they look like, are looking for the same thing," President Obama wrote. "They're not trying to get filthy rich. They don't expect someone else to do what they can do for themselves.

"But they do expect that if they're willing to work, they should be able to find a job that supports a family. They expect that they shouldn't go bankrupt just because they get sick. They expect that their kids should be able to get a good education, one that prepares them for this new economy, and they should be able to afford college if they've put in the effort. They want to be safe, from criminals and terrorists. And they figure that after a lifetime of work, they should be able to retire with dignity and respect."

Every workplace should have its own version of this type of articulation of core ambition. Few do. Many workplaces talk about their visions. Few really articulate the core of why they exist.

In many of the places I have worked, there have been considerable efforts to change culture. There have been culture groups, cultural change programs, cultural consultants and cultural workshops.

Some of these things are useful in getting people thinking about culture and setting in motion some shared discipline around shared behaviours and creating safe environments.

Having said that, the places I have worked with really strong, positive work cultures, did not ever mention culture. The culture was strong because the organisation hired the right people and the right leaders. Culture was not created, it existed.

In my experience, the following attributes have defined workplaces and organisations with exemplary culture.

- They only hire people who share the values and contribute to the culture.
- They provide a genuine, safe environment where people feel empowered to have an opinion. There are genuine robust conversations and debate without anyone feeling insulted.
- They have leaders with the confidence to trust and delegate.

- Innovation is a mindset rather than a "thing" that needs to be discussed.
- The organisation genuinely cares about its people and recognises that they are humans with foibles and faults.
- People work really hard, but the company recognises that employees have a life outside of work. People feel empowered to go home and shut off work at the end of the day.

So, back to my sister's school debate on whether there is an Australian culture. Her team had the affirmative side and argued that there was not "an" (as in one) Australian culture, but many. They won.

I disagreed with the argument because multiple cultures can still create a single collective culture with its own, unique attributes. But their approach did highlight the multiple voices and backgrounds that come together to form a collective.

As the song *We Are Australian* goes, "we are one, but we are many…we share a dream and sing with one voice." In any situation, bringing different people together to sing with one voice feels powerful and comforting. Being part of a great culture is a truly uplifting experience.

13. The traits of great leaders

The writing of human history seems largely based around an obsession with leaders. For good reason.

There are billions of people in the world but somehow a small number step up to lead the way and give our otherwise bumbling species a sense of direction and order.

Leaders come in all forms. Some lead countries. Some lead great armies. Some lead through respect and genius. Some just have an innate ability to attract followers.

Leadership is often confused with hierarchy and titles. Real leaders do not need titles. They lead because something about them gives people confidence. They have some special "it" factor that other humans recognise and gravitate towards.

We also have leaders for the times. Leaders of countries and states tend to reflect a collective view of what is needed. Sometimes we go for hard-nosed leaders who make big, risky calls and get things done quickly.

Other times we go with consensus-style leaders who aim to bring everybody along and give everyone a stake in the outcome.

In democracies, populations tend to have a good sense of what is needed, particularly the swinging voters in the middle who are not wedded to a doctrine of the left or the right.

In the corporate world, leaders have developed something of a cult following. Prior to the 1980s, most people could barely name a handful of company leaders. Now we have dozens of superstar entrepreneurs who are pushing the boundaries of technology and finding bold new ways to navigate business at the speed of change.

There has been much written about the new breed of leaders. The story goes that contemporary leadership requires emotional intelligence, charisma and the ability to empower others.

Contemporary leaders do not get "caught in the weeds". They know the difference between leadership and management. They make "big bets" and take a helicopter view of the company.

They encourage innovation, they bring talented people through the ranks at any age and they create workplaces that are invigorating and supportive.

All these are great attributes. They also require something akin to superpowers and set enormous expectations that are hard to sustain.

These superpower expectations probably help to explain why the tenure of CEOs of large companies is reducing.

The 2018 CEO Success study by Pricewaterhousecoopers showed the CEO churn rate rose to a record 17.5% in that year (the highest in the study's 19 years). CEOs had a median tenure of five years and less than one in five stayed in the role more than 10 years.

This could be reflective of a greater propensity in general for people to change jobs more often. It could be that the pressure on CEOs is so great that five years is a long stint. It could be that the expectations are so great that very few humans can keep owners and shareholders happy for long periods.

Over a long career, I have worked with many leaders – a few bad ones, a lot of good ones, a tiny number of great ones.

There was a remarkable consistency in the traits of the bad, good and great ones.

Traits of bad leaders

- They do not listen
- They are poor communicators
- They are moody and inconsistent
- They blame others for their bad decisions
- They have zero tolerance for mistakes
- They micromanage and don't trust anyone
- They encourage factions
- They have obvious "class pets"
- They listen to the wrong people
- Their core loyalty does not sit with their people
- They tolerate or even encourage toxic behaviour
- They make half-baked decisions
- They lack genuine empathy for people

Traits of good leaders

- They have a clear strategy and a plan to deliver it
- They hire good people and listen to them

- They create a safe environment for people to have an opinion and contribute to conversations
- They genuinely encourage and support diversity in the workplace
- They communicate what is going on and why decisions are made
- They have solid rules and guidelines, and their companies operate efficiently
- They run good meetings that produce results
- They celebrate and reward success
- They have strong people and culture systems to deal with workplace performance
- They have a growth mentality and the confidence to make investments
- They have a good relationship with the board or owners and employees can trust them to get the backing they need
- They provide professional and personal development for their staff
- They pay people fairly
- They encourage hard work but not overly long hours and "facetime"
- They are "family friendly"

Traits of great leaders

- They are genuinely inspiring, and they attract other inspiring people
- They think at least 10 years ahead and there is a genuine forward program of ideas and innovation

- They intuitively understand the prevailing global and local context and seamlessly sync the company to that
- They focus on the big picture, but they take the time to really listen to people and understand what is happening in their lives
- They have real relationships at all levels of the organisation
- They have time and space in their week – they don't just do meetings
- They encourage "big" conversations beyond today's business as usual issue
- Woman and minority groups are well represented in all areas of their organisation without any programs or affirmative action to achieve that
- Their people work hard but also work flexible hours without needing to ask permission
- Their company constantly implements new ideas and better ways without ever using the "I" word (innovation)
- They give people strong direction but then get out of their way and let them deliver
- They totally empower their people to make decisions
- They provide real incentives for people to do well
- They back their people even when they make mistakes
- They have good systems and guidelines, but they are so simple and intuitive that nobody ever talks about them

- They encourage highly robust and respectful discussions where people can have a strong view without negative consequences
- They deal with toxic people quickly and decisively (in fact the culture is so strong that it destroys any toxin that enters the ecosystem)

The leaders who display the "great" traits do not all look the same or come from similar backgrounds. They are often vastly different in many respects. Some grow up in poverty, some in great wealth. Some have childhoods with no hints of their leadership abilities. Others are "born leaders" their whole lives.

Some never talk or think about "leadership". Others are students of leadership and collect and implement traits as they develop.

All the really great ones make it look easy.

Frankly, leadership is not for everyone. Many people feel pressured to take on leadership jobs when they know they are ill-suited for them. Even intelligent and highly successful people are often more content to follow than lead. Deep down we all know if we are comfortable at the front or in the pack.

Despite the clichés around new leadership requirements, I am not sure the basic traits of successful leadership have really changed much.

While we are less likely to celebrate hard-nosed, hierarchy-style leaders in the 21st Century, many of the great leaders of history were characterised by the same greatness that still epitomises our truly successful leaders.

Great leaders have always inspired us and found ways to unite us around ideas that make sense and we can feel part of. Bully leaders with poor human attributes and an obsession with their own power tend to have limited shelf lives and are treated poorly in recorded history.

Leading is a privilege and a title means little. You cannot lead without followers.

14. The search for truth

For most of my childhood, my parents were in search of a song. They heard it on the radio once and looked for it every time they went to a record store.

When I left home at 21 the song remained elusive.

This was back in the days when the Internet was just a glint in a dreamer's eye. You couldn't Google a song to find it. You just stayed vigilant for the possibility of discovery. You had to be patient.

The evasive song was called *What is Truth?* by country singer Johnny Cash.

The childhood quest for *What is Truth?* helped trigger a lifelong curiosity about the nature of truth. It is a surprisingly intriguing, challenging and deep question.

What is truth? No, really. Do we know any more?

It seems that establishing the contemporary definition of truth has become something of an all-pervasive global preoccupation.

Anything we disagree with can be written off as "fake news". Everyone has access to "media" and vast audiences. We don't really know if we can trust information or not. We don't know if it has been checked or if it is deliberately misleading. Even photographic "evidence" could be an illusion conjured through Photoshop.

In this world, it seems that every day the truth gets a little harder to find.

The truth dilemma came back to me starkly in 2021 when I watched a Netflix documentary called *The Social Dilemma*.

In a nutshell it highlights the concerns of some very smart people (many of whom were instrumental in developing social media in Silicon Valley) that social media is creating societal subsets of likeminded people who congregate in digital enclaves and just reinforce their own world view to each other. This happens without the checks and balances of objectivity or alternative voices.

This can cause extreme, and even dangerous versions of "the truth" to take hold in vast numbers with potentially dire consequences for our social cohesion and systems of democracy.

According to the documentary, the new world of social media also allows mass manipulation of information and people, with few checks and balances and very loose rulesets around what is real, ethical and reasonable.

Sadly, the documentary itself does exactly what it is highlighting as potentially dangerous. It interviews only people with effectively the same views on the issue. As a former "old-school" journalist I found myself craving the alternative view, which clearly exists, so I could have a more informed opinion.

It seems that the growth of digital tribes is just one of the manifestations of an assault on the truth that was seeded decades ago.

When I started in journalism in the 1980s, so-called "spin" was in its infancy as a science. In the years hence it has grown in manpower, sophistication and infiltration.

Information that is "spun" is not necessarily wrong. It is simply distorted towards a version of the facts that favours a particular viewpoint or outcome. Sometimes this encourages healthy debate. Sometimes it just suppresses relevant facts.

Adding to this, much of the remnants of what we used to call mainstream or mass media now unashamedly sits in a philosophical paddock rather than on the fence where it once resided.

The trends even have me questioning the very nature of a "universal truth". As a child when we wanted to assert something as true, we claimed it to be a "scientific fact". As you get older you realise that even scientists disagree on what constitutes a fact. For every learned study there seems to be another one with totally contradictory results.

As a journalist you quickly learn the nuanced nature of truth. Most of us went into journalism because we wanted to find the truth and use it to improve the world.

Quickly this becomes more complicated. You talk to someone and the facts that they present leave you outraged, and you set out to right the wrong. Until you talk to the person at the other side of the issue who has an equally plausible, and totally opposing take.

Over time you start to wonder if a single truth is out there at all. Is it as simple as right or wrong or do most situations revolve around the same set of circumstances viewed through different lenses, from different vantage points and from different backgrounds? "One man's trash is another man's treasure."

For all of its faults, journalism in its heyday had a lot of checks and balances. Hardened senior editors would question everything and set a high bar on truth and proof well before a story was published. At least four and up to seven people checked everything before it went live.

Even then we used to lament what former colleague, the late Peter Charlton, termed "degrees of inadequacy". In other words, despite the best attempts at objectivity and best-intended quest for the truth, we were only as good as the time we had and the information we could access.

In our new world of truth pulled and manipulated in hundreds of directions like Mr Fantastic in the *Fantastic Four*, even the recording of our history becomes problematic.

A librarian told me once that written history was riddled with errors because a journalist got it wrong at some point in time and the inaccuracy then was cleansed and legitimised in authoritative text.

Imagine using today's vast number of online words as the basis for history. Future historians may well conclude that the world in the 2020s was ruled by Instagram bikini model influencers and our "monarchs" were determined on the *The Bachelor*.

Personally, I'm not ready to give up on the truth even if it ultimately proves to be a holy grail that is eventually written off as a myth.

I didn't give up on looking for the *What is Truth?* song either. When I was in my 30s I was flicking through a CD discount bin. I picked up a Johnny Cash CD and there it was! I had to look at it many times to convince myself it was real.

By then my Mum had died way too young without ever hearing the song again but I bought the CD and gave it to my Dad. He just gave an incredulous smile and shook his head. We had completed a quest that had long ago fallen into the background of our lives.

We listened to the song (recorded in 1971) together in silence.

The old man turned off the radio.
Said, "Where did all of the old songs go?
Kids sure play funny music these days.
They play it in the strangest ways."
Said, "It looks to me like they've all gone wild.
It was peaceful back when I was a child."
Well, man, could it be that the girls and boys
Are trying to be heard above your noise?
And the lonely voice of youth cries "What is truth?"

Maybe things have not changed so much after all.

SECTION 5

Finding the life you imagined

"There is no passion to be found playing small – in settling for a life that is less than the one you are capable of living."
- **Nelson Mandela** (former South African president)

This final section is about that crazy little thing called life. It is such an individual thing yet, the more I connect with people around the world, the more I realise how much commonality we have with our basic aspirations and challenges.

Whatever life we choose to live, we all leave an imprint in the universe. Millions have come before us and millions will follow us. All we can do is live the life we are given and do our best to leave an imprint worthy of the gift of existence.

Everyone's life is different. These are my reflections on work and life, its challenges and finding our unique place in the world.

1. Avoiding burnout

My wife would tell you that I am the worst person on the planet to give advice on avoiding burnout. My name is Shane Rodgers and I have hit burn-out a lot over the years. This is the first time I have felt comfortable admitting it and writing about it.

It started when I was at school. I liked doing so many things. Soon I found myself putting my hand up for every job, producing school newspapers, doing debating and public speaking, writing and performing plays and joining every community group that my age allowed. I was school captain and student council president, and I have lost count of how many sports I played. This was on top of working to maintain good marks at school.

This meant busy days, busy nights, busy weekends. Busy always.

I got away with it for a while. Kids have boundless energy and enormous capacity to go hard and then sleep deep. It started to change in high school. In most years of my high schooling, I got to about November at full pace and then hit a wall. Typically, I was off school for a week or two with something that was probably a virus, given a free run at my body because of its exhausted state.

This unsustainable pace carried over into my working life. It manifested in long hours, bringing work home on the weekends, producing documents and strategies in my "free" time and almost never saying no to internal and external requests for my time.

This was on top of having small children, doing a long commute to work and mostly living on acreage with an unrelenting maintenance schedule. I convinced myself that I was Superman, possessed of some enormous ability to keep producing without proper rest and always in top gear.

I was wrong.

In my 20s and 30s I got away with it to a point. Mostly I was okay. However, I barely got away with a single year without my annual dose of burn-out virus. Sometimes it happened in winter. Sometimes I was the only person I knew with a November-December summer "flu".

I was well into my 40s before the proverbial chickens started to come home to roost. A routine corporate health check revealed my blood pressure was high. It got tested a few times. It was always high.

I asked the doctors for some time to get it down rather than going straight to medication. I tried more exercise, herbs, something from a South American tree root, meditation, trying to get more sleep and more rest on the weekend. Nothing worked.

I hated the idea of being on long-term medication, but the doctor said it was basically a choice between medication or dying young of a stroke. I chose life.

There is seldom any precise reasons given for high blood pressure. It can be hereditary, a product of poor lifestyle or related to bad relationships and long-term stress. Or a combination.

Generally, I tried to convince myself that mine was hereditary. Deep down I knew that was not the full answer. The body is simply not designed to run in top gear all the time. Over the years mine forgot how to find low gear. It just kept running at high gear until the engine blew up and needed to go into the mechanic for maintenance.

You would think that a realisation of being in a burn-out cycle would be enough to do something about it. It helps but, like any addiction, it is hard to break.

In my case, the older I get the longer it takes to recover from each period of burnout. In 2015 I contracted a virus that had me bed-ridden for six weeks. It attacked my middle ear, my stomach, my head and my pelvis. I couldn't walk and I couldn't sleep because the heartbeat in my head was too loud.

I kept going to the doctor and they tested me for everything. In the end they concluded that it was viral, my immune system was weak from a long run of exhaustion and viruses, and I would just have to wait it out. Eventually it went away but it took nearly two years to really feel normal again.

I worked harder at slowing down and resting in the following years but, in 2020, the engine started over-revving again and I couldn't wind it back. Sure enough, I hit November and ended up in hospital for several days with chronic pain, very low blood pressure and severe lethargy. I had head scans, MRIs and bone scans. They showed nothing that would explain the symptoms. I was out of action for two weeks and really tired for weeks afterwards. Doctors found it baffling. For me, it was a familiar scenario.

More recently I had tests that revealed that sometime in the past I had a "silent heart attack" – one I survived and did not identify at the time. Thankfully my prognosis and general health are sound. However, for someone who once believed he was bulletproof, it was a heck of a wakeup call.

I guess this whole sorry scenario raises the question of why. I am far from alone in suffering over-work syndrome and many of you reading this will be early in your career and already noticing the behaviour.

On reflection, I think there are quite a few things at play. The most powerful (and the hardest to admit) is getting addicted to people thinking you have some sort of superhuman capacity. Through this you can become addicted to praise and start using it as a drug to constantly verify your worth.

When I was a young political journalist in the Canberra Press Gallery in Australia in the 1980s and 1990s, I produced so many stories that I was nicknamed "prolific". Once you have that nickname, you feel the need to constantly live up to it.

As chief-of-staff of a national news bureau during that same period, I would get up at 5.30am and read about nine newspapers and then monitor all the morning radio and television. By the time most of the other journalists started work around 10am I was across everything going on and people knew they could rely on me to ensure nothing fell through the cracks. Again, once you set that standard, it is hard to walk away or change without a deep feeling that you are disappointing others.

Largely due to my early years in the Canberra Press Gallery, I have an enormous ability to assess information at lightning speed and produce reports quickly and accurately. There is little need to do that anymore, but I still tend to do it.

I once produced a 450-page very detailed national market assessment for an employer in four weeks. Everyone was astounded that anyone could produce this report in such a short time. Secretly I enjoyed that. Within two hours of delivering it, I got November "flu" and stayed in bed for 10 days. You get the idea.

If you find yourself with the same syndrome, you really need to address it. The impact on your body gets worse as you get older and if you never address it, it almost certainly will impact on your quality and longevity of life.

If you are highly capable and you have a strong work ethic, one of the hardest things to do is give yourself permission to slow down and work at normal human pace. And once you have trained yourself to move at super pace, a slower pace comes with an almost crippling sense of guilt.

There are lots of good reasons to treat a burn-out cycle as a major problem that needs urgent remedy. Your health is the most obvious and the most important. You also need to be aware of the impact it has on your family and friends. People watch you burning out and feel powerless to help or do anything about it.

The irony of "super work" is that it doesn't necessarily help your career. It can relegate you to senior, responsible jobs, but not the top job. The top job goes to smart people who marshal the smart, prolific people but give themselves the clear air and thinking time to lead properly without getting caught in the weeds.

If you think you are caught in this work addiction, you really should deal with it as early as possible. Do not think it will happen automatically. You need to make a difficult, proactive choice and work at it like every other hard choice.

2. The meaning of life

It does not pay to spend too much time pondering the nature of the universe. The universe is so vast and mind-blowing that it defies comprehension.

On many levels, it is a genuinely scary proposition – the distance, the large vacuums of eerie silence and the mystery of whether there is other life out there. And if there is will it be friendly like in *Cocoon* or terrifying like

Alien? Life Jim but not as we know it (to quote *Star Trekking across the Universe*).

Then there is our own little blue planet that fluked a prime space in the universe and supported a freak genetic sequence that over many, many years produced humans – a species with the incredible ability to use and manipulate its surroundings in extraordinary ways.

Even on this aberration of a planet there is only a relatively small area ideal for human life. Climate change science suggests that even this small area is under real threat. In the years ahead, the usable space may get very cosy (and perhaps dangerous).

Then there is the question of whether humans have earnt the right to inhabit the universe forever, or whether we are a tiny anomaly in the vast universe that will be a mere blip in time, only to become a relic of history floating along in a galaxy lost in the vastness of dead empty space.

At any time, we are probably only an asteroid hit, serious pandemic, or nuclear war away from total extinction. We may be steadily destroying the planet and have set ourselves on an unsustainable path based on economic success for now, rather than maintaining our race for hundreds of thousands more years.

To quote comedian George Carlin, the planet might eventually decide that we are a "surface nuisance" and find a way to exterminate us.

Sometimes, it really does not pay to go there.

In the TV series *Sherlock* (based on the Sir Arthur Conan Doyle Sherlock Holmes detective stories) the Holmes character, played by Benedict Cumberbatch, is genuinely brilliant. Yet his offsider John Watson is flabbergasted that Sherlock knows so little about the solar system or that the earth orbits around the Sun. "What does it matter," Sherlock logics. "So, we go 'round the sun', If we went 'round the moon or round and round the garden like a teddy bear it wouldn't make any difference."

Pointing to his head, he explains: "This is my hard drive and it only makes sense to put things in there that are useful. Really useful. Ordinary people fill their heads with all kinds of rubbish. And that makes it hard to get at the stuff that matters."

Sherlock is perhaps a bit extreme on these things, but the point is well made. Our brains can become quickly overstretched if we think we need to understand everything.

We don't. And somehow nature, as a human collective, seems to produce enough of the right people who understand almost everything, and are prepared to do every role. Mostly we are better off leaving expertise to the experts and devoting our efforts to understanding our own place in the world and the expertise we bring to the collective.

In younger years I was guilty of believing that I needed to be able to do everything. It bothered me that I could not speak more languages or fix cars or perform brain surgery. It bothered me that there were things I did not know and may never know.

I even worried about not being able to visit every country and city in the world in the course of my lifetime. Somehow, I felt an obligation to do that, even though there was no logic to it.

It has taken me many years to accept that I don't need to know the meaning of life in its larger, big universe, forces of nature, million-year history sense.

All I really need to understand is the meaning of my own life. That is challenging enough.

I sometimes deliberately scare myself by lying on the bed and just saying over and over in my head: "I really am me." It sounds a bit ridiculous but when I did this for the first time at the age of 10 it terrified me so much that I broke out in a cold sweat.

After a few minutes of repeating this line I suddenly get this stark realisation that my life is real and the person I see in the mirror is me. My brain is where my consciousness resides, and it is controlling the body through a combination of conscious and unconscious actions. There also comes a realisation that you cannot sit out life. You are in it. You need to keep moving and work out what you want to do with it every day.

Simple? Yes. An unnerving thought? Also yes.

I'm sure there is a solid psychological reason for this sensation, and I have no idea if it would impact everyone the same way. For me it seems to have something to do with our brain being something of a pilot for our body (think the Eddie Murphy robot in the movie *Meet Dave*).

WORKNADO

We take for granted how it all works but we don't spend a lot of time accepting the true reality of that.

Inside our heads we have our two speed brains – frontal cortex for things we are doing now and the database in the back to feed everything we do and store our learnings and instincts.

Then we have our physical body which carries us around but is also the means by which we engage with other humans and how we are perceived in the context of looks, race, body language, physical skills and language.

On top of that we are overlayed with an even more mysterious side that relies more on faith and a belief system than science. Depending on where you sit in that spectrum, this can be seen as consciousness (apparently unique to humans), a soul or some other type of spiritual condition that defies logical explanation in the context of our current knowledge base.

The human condition is complicated. And simple.

If you put the complexity aside the meaning of life is simple. We are here to do our bit. We are here to understand what skills we have to enhance the world as it is and help to improve it.

We are here to be part of a community and a society and to help ensure that fellow humans are supported and valued.

We are here to work with others so the whole becomes greater than sum of the parts.

We are here to have and raise children to perpetuate the human species (where that is possible and makes sense) or to help and protect our young people so they have the opportunity to reach their potential and help create a better future.

We are here to work together to find better ways and to build a world that is not only sustainable into the future but continues to improve and prosper.

We are here to create things that did not exist before – writing, film, video, art, inventions – using the unique skills that each of us have.

In the end, it does not really matter if human life was created through a chaotic scientific sequence or by a guiding hand. What matters is that we have life. It is all we have. It is precious. It needs to be treasured and preserved.

If we value our lives and live them well, with gratitude, kindness and empathy, our lives will have meaning. If our own lives have meaning, this will be contagious.

3. Working out why you were put on earth

"People are always blaming their circumstances for what they are. I don't believe in circumstances. The people who get on in this world are the people who get up and look for the circumstances they want, and, if they can't find them, make them."
 - **George Bernard Shaw** (Irish playwright)

So here we are in the Worknado with forces of change swirling around us and our lives being carried along in an unrelenting slipstream of time.

Each day we wake to a new sunrise and we are gifted an allocation of hours in which to carry out our lives.

We are all products of historical luck. If any of our direct ancestors got hit by a bus (or perhaps a large horse) at any time in thousands of years, we would not exist.

We have no choice on where we are born or the circumstances we are born into.

We have little control over who (out of the billions of people in the world) will interact with us during our lives. Our circle is ultimately small, our place in time and history is fleeting and we are the product of a miracle of existence too extraordinary to fathom.

Yet here we are with our gift of time, the day we wake up to every day and, if we are lucky, a fair degree of choice on how to use what we have been given.

Deciding what to do with our time gift it is the most important decision we make. Living a life of fulfilment interspersed with some genuine joy is our most cherished aspiration.

Almost everyone knows deep down that they have a passion or an "element" that truly defines them. Yet how often do people put their dreams or their passions on hold because reality bites? As a result, they live every day with slight feelings of regret and a gnawing sense that they are usually at the wrong station waiting for the wrong train.

In a world with so many possibilities, most of us worry

that there is something else out there for us that we are missing. Some people go on long sabbaticals to "find" themselves. People who are hugely successful in business start charities to help change the world or "give back". Everyone seems to be searching for meaning outside of the curse of routine.

If we are lucky, we can find our true passion and turn it into a career. That is not always possible. Sometimes we need to do something different to pay the bills. But that should not stop us putting our passions at the centre of our lives.

As I said earlier in this book, during my years in senior management roles at News Corporation, I was regularly asked how you "break into" journalism. My answer was always that you did not need to rely on someone else to do that. Declare yourself a journalist today and start writing. You may have to do something else to earn money for a while but that is no reason to put your passion on hold waiting for someone else to legitimise it.

The same is true for anything. We all have the right to declare who we are and be that person. In the evolution of nature, we all have something unique and special to contribute to the inelegant, haphazard and largely unpredictable procession of society.

As renowned psychologist Abraham Maslow said: "A musician must make music, an artist must paint, a poet must write, if he is to be ultimately at peace with himself. What one can be, one must be." Our world is a wilderness garden in which each plant fights a relentless battle for sustenance and growth, but the result is somehow methodical, and beautiful. The process is chaos, yet somehow the result appears ordered and guided.

We make everyone's life better when we use our special talents to advance the tasks we are good at. The small ripple we put in the vastness of history and the universe can form a wave. Something that we say or write can be passed along through thousands of years and enrich a moment for a stranger we will never know in a future we will never experience.

As I sit and contemplate life, I often try to strip away the day to day "stuff" to find what really lies beneath.

I am struck by the periods of life that now seem like an oil painting. The people existed and the events happened, but children grow, people move away and pass away, paint fades, buildings collapse, jobs churn.

Our past is a phantasmagoria of memories seemingly stored randomly by our brains; whole days we will never recall, faces now wiped of names, moments starved of context, feelings ripped so deep that they occasionally rise mysteriously to the surface unprompted.

Sometimes we have periods of life where the stars line up. But they seldom stay in alignment for long. The forces of change are juggernauts that no human can defy. We can capture moments in a photograph but by the time the camera is clicked, the moment is already passing. Then it exists entombed in a frame, captured for eternity, yet somehow still gone forever.

In *The career advice I had at 25* (the LinkedIn article that started the Worknado journey) I talked about the time machine we would have in the future to go back and talk to our younger selves.

In fact, that time machine already exists. It just does not take us back. It takes us forward. Every day I am using insights garnered by my 25-year-old self and applying learnings that my stumbling 3-year-old-self loaded into a hyper receptive brain.

My 35-year-old-self cautions me against overdoing things. My 40-year-old-self reminds me to stop and smell the roses.

The people who have come and gone have enriched my existence with their time and perspectives. Their imprint is still tangible, and the universe still holds a place for them.

At any juncture, we are a product of a maelstrom of genetic evolution, experiences, environments, and random forces that unconsciously shape us.

The Worknado is not new. Throughout history mankind has coped with challenges and emerged with learnings and strength that have benefited those of us who have followed.

I may never know what I was put on earth to do, and that may well be the point. There is little value in going forward or back. All we can really do is make the best of now and try to be true to ourselves and make the best contribution we can.

If the end-of-life report card says: "Always tried his best" I will be good with that. As my dad always says, all you can ever do is your best.

"The greatest danger for most of us is not that our aim is too high, and we miss it, but that it is too low, and we reach it."
    -**Michelangelo** (artist)

References

The following books are referenced in *Worknado*

1. Achor, Shawn. *The happiness advantage: The seven principles of positive psychology that fuel success and performance at work.* Virgin, 2010.
2. Achor, Shawn. *Before happiness.* Currency, 2013.
3. Bryson, Bill. *A Short History of Nearly Everything.* Crown, 2004.
4. Ware, Bronnie, *The Top Five Regrets of the Dying*, Hay House, 2012.
5. Collins, J. C. *Good to great: Why some companies make the leap...and others don't.* New York, Harper Business, 2001.
6. Frankl, Viktor E. *Man's Search for Meaning: an Introduction to Logotherapy.* Boston, Beacon Press, 1962.
7. Gladwell, Malcolm. *Outliers: The Story of Success.* New York, Little, Brown and Co., 2008.
8. Gratton, Linda & Scott, Andrew. *The 100-Year Life.* Bloomsbury Information, 2016.
9. Koch, Richard, *The 80/20 Principle.* Broadway Business, 1999.
10. Obama, Barack. *A Promised Land.* Crown, 2020.
11. Robinson, K., & Aronica, L. *The element: How finding your passion changes everything.* New York: Penguin Group USA, 2009.
12. Rodgers, Shane. *Tall People Don't Jump: The curious behaviour of human beings*, Createspace, 2014.
13. Soojung-Kim Pang, Alex. *Rest: Why you get more done when you work less.* Basic Books, 2016.
14. Traill, Michael. *Jumping Ship.* Sydney, Hardie Grant, 2016

ABOUT THE AUTHOR

Shane Rodgers is a business leader, strategist and astute observer of human behaviour.

His insightful, witty, and unassuming style has allowed him to enjoy a successful career leading and mentoring hundreds of people, while helping to reboot the fortunes of national companies.

A former colleague once referred to Shane as "the oracle" because he has the unique ability to cut through the BS and get to the heart of the matter.

He wrote *Worknado* to help anyone who has ever struggled to fulfil their career goals and aspirations and still live a complete and satisfying life.

Shane's university-level qualifications are in economics and history. He began his career as a journalist and editor specialising in the workplace, social change and economics.

In his mid-20s, Shane was propelled into senior management roles. He practices what he preaches and was able to successfully transition into a C-suite career – specialising in new business models, organisational structures, strategy, social change, marketing, and branding.

He has served in senior executive positions in nearly 20 organisations from media, universities, and not-for-profit to government departments, economic development agencies, and business membership organisations.

Shane lives in Australia. His writing has attracted a strong global following.

WORKNADO

Printed in Great Britain
by Amazon